Out of the Box or Inside the Book?

Companies brag about their latest product being the result of "thinking out of the box." Doing something that common "inside-the-box" thinking would not allow them to do. They pat themselves on the back for this creative achievement. For them, "thinking out of the box" is profitable.

Sadly, "out of the box" thinking – when it comes to the Holy Bible, God's love letter to us; with answers to key questions: Where did we come from? Who created our world and the universe? And how was it created? – has become a global epidemic.

Fewer of us in today's world look for answers "Inside the Book" as we've sold out to the "scientific" approach of today. It is an approach, in our opinion, that has lost the objective search for truth to which the founders of scientific fields adhered. Today if scientists and scholars express that objectivity – and hold to traditional Biblical-based beliefs in Creation *Ex Nihilo* – they are criticized and sometimes fired.

It's to the point where if we do not bow to the dictates of what we call "shallow science," we are scorned.

"The Bible is true word for word and cover to cover."
Russ Miller, Creation, Evolution & Science Ministries

The problem with the "scientific" approach of today, we constrain science to have a naturalistic foundation, but eliminate the possibility of finding truth because the truth may be a supernatural explanation. To find the entire truth, we must take off all constraints.

In the process of finding the correct interpretation, we take the whole Bible – Genesis to Revelation – into account in coming to an understanding and correct interpretation of what is written.

We read and reread as well as meditate upon the scriptures and continue to grow in the Word. What we believe the scriptures are saying might be different than what we thought two years ago. As we grow in the Lord, we are allowed to change our mind.

The Bible is a living book, and Jesus is the Life. He gives us the Holy Spirit so that we can read the Book and understand the Book.

Let's try to live "Inside the Book" as much as we can.

Suzanne Sawyer Vincent, author and Jim Dobkins, publisher

No Gap.
No Chaos.

Answers for Creation *Ex Nihilo* Naysayers.

Suzanne Sawyer Vincent

No Gap. No Chaos.
Answers for Creation *Ex Nihilo* Naysayers.

Suzanne Sawyer Vincent

Published by UCS Press
UCS PRESS is an imprint of MarJim Books
PO Box 12797
Prescott, AZ 86304-2797

Cover design by Marti Dobkins

ISBN 978-0-943247-80-9

PUBLISHER'S NOTE: Although some Bible translations do not capitalize pronouns of God the Father, God the Son or God the Holy Spirit, for the sake of reverence to our Creator, and also to have consistent word usage throughout this book, we have used capital beginning letters for such pronouns; for example, Him, His, He.

Dedication

To three persons who have stood in the midst of opposition. Ellen Myers (1925-) wrote many years for Creation Social Science and Humanities Quarterly of Wichita, KS and is still active in creation work. Rev. Walter Lang (1913-2004), Lutheran minister, founded Bible-Science Association in 1963. Art Katz (1929-2007) founded Ben Israel Community in 1975.

Acknowledgement

To Jim and Marti Dobkins, editors premiere.

Table of Contents

Preface..7
Chapter 1 Genesis 1:1 and 1:2 11
  1a. Beginning... 11
  1b. Heavens 19
  1c. Heaven and Earth... 26
  1d. Angels.. 36
  1e. Earth... 40
  1f. Sabbath.. 49
Chapter 2 Creation *Ex Nihilo* 55
  2a. Creation of Heavenly Heavens and Cosmos
     on Day One.. 60
  2b. Were Angels Created before Genesis 1:1 or
     Outside Time? 62
  2c. Traditional View (Originally Perfect
     Yet Incomplete Theory) 63
Chapter 3 Chaos Before Creation of Universe 69
  3a. Greek Philosophers.. 69
  3b. Gnosticism and Nicolaitans................................ 71
  3c. Precreation Chaos (Modified Gap)...................... 76
Chapter 4 Gap Theories.. 80
  4a. Ruin-Restitution Gap 81
  4b. Undefined Age Biblical Literalists...................... 88
  4c. Some Traditionalists 90
  4d. Re-creation Revelation Theory 91
Chapter 5 Early Creed 94
  5a. Early Church and Apostle Paul 94
  5b. Early Church Fathers... 98
  5c. Jewish Scholars near Time of Jesus 103
Chapter 6 Summary.. 107
List of Authors or Works 110
List of Words or Terms... 117
References.. 123

Preface

Portions of this work were presented at the 4th Creation Research Society meeting held August 8-9, 2014 in Petersburg, Kentucky (Vincent 2014). This book is divided into six chapters and references. The subdivisions of the chapters are entitled sections.

I have considered four overriding principles to be very important when commenting on truths obtained from studying the Bible. The principles are listed below with scriptural passages to authenticate them. I would appreciate you reading over the scriptures given here to help you understand better the task that I have undertaken.

Principle number 1. There is simplicity in the gospel of Jesus Christ.

II Corinthians 11:3 states there is a simplicity that is in Christ (also translated sincere and pure devotion).

I Corinthians 14:33 states for God is not a God of disorder but of peace (also translated God is not the author of confusion).

Luke 18:17 says anyone who does not receive the kingdom of God like a little child will never enter it.

Principle number 2. The Holy Spirit will lead us into all truth. Related to that, you must be born again to see the kingdom of God.

John 3:3 says no one can see the kingdom of God unless he is born again (also translated born from above).

John 14:16-17 says He [Father] shall give us another Comforter, that He may abide with you forever; even the Spirit of truth.

John 14:26 states but the Comforter, which is the Holy Ghost, whom the father will send in my name, He shall teach you all things.

I Corinthians 2:14 says the man without the spirit cannot understand spiritual truths, because they are spiritually discerned.

I Corinthians 2 explains that the mind of Christ is the Spirit who searches all things even the deep things of God.

Principle number 3. Be careful not to multiply words without knowledge. God warns at the end of Revelation that nothing should be added or taken away from the Holy Scripture. Related to that is testing the spirit of any teaching to see if it is from God or the enemy.

Principle number 3, not multiplying words.

Job 35:16 says so Job opened his mouth with empty talk; without knowledge he multiplies words.

Job 34:35 states Job has spoken without knowledge and his words were without wisdom.

Job 42:3 says therefore have I uttered that I understand not; things too wonderful for me, which I knew not.

Psalm 131:1 says neither do I exercise myself in great matters, or things too high for me.

And *Jude 16* says ...and their mouths speaketh great swelling words, having men's persons in admiration because of advantage.

Principle number 3, not adding or subtracting from Scripture.

Revelation 22:18-19 states do not add to this book or take words away from this book of prophecy.

Proverbs 30:6 states add thou not unto His words, lest He reprove thee, and thou be found a liar. *Deuteronomy 4:2* states you shall not add unto the word which I command you, neither shall you diminish ought from it.

Deuteronomy 12:32 thou shall not add thereto, nor diminish from it.

Romans 10:2 says the Israelites sought to establish their own [righteousness], they did not submit to God's righteousness.

Mark 7:7 they worship Me in vain; their teachings are but rules taught by men.

Mark 7:9 states and He said to them: "you have a fine way of setting aside the commands of God in order to observe your own traditions!"

John 5:39 says you diligently study the Scriptures because you think that by them you possess eternal life. These are the Scriptures that testify about Me, yet you refuse to come to Me to have life.

Colos*sians 2:8* says beware lest any man spoil you through philosophy and vain deceit, after the tradition of men, after the rudiments of the world, and not after Christ.

And *I Timothy 6:20* says avoiding profane and vain babblings, and oppositions of science falsely so called.

Principle number 3, testing the spirits

Matthew 7:15 says Beware of false prophets, which come to you in sheep's clothing, but inwardly they are ravening wolves.

Colossians 2:18 says Let no man beguile you… intruding into those things which he has seen . . .

I John 4:1 says Beloved, believe not every spirit, but try the spirits whether they are of God: because many false prophets are gone out in the world.

Principle number 4. The gospel is to the Jew first, then to the Gentile. Related to that, we Christians honor the Old Testament. To the Hebrews were given the Hebrew letters, the covenant, the temple services, the promises, and the prophecies.

John 4:22 says we know what we worship, for salvation is of the Jews.

Romans 1:16 says for it [gospel of Christ] is the power of God unto salvation to everyone that believeth, to the Jew first, and also to the Greek.

Romans 11:24 says how much more readily will these, the natural branches, be grafted into their own olive tree!

Romans 9:5 says theirs [Israelites] are the patriarchs, and from them is traced the human ancestry of Christ who is God over all, forever praised. Amen!

Related to these four principles is having peace in our heart as the Scriptures are read and interpreted with the help of the Holy Spirit. Caution is needed as commentaries written by various Christian theologians and Jewish Midrash or other writings are read. Discretion is needed when considering their interpretations. Many men and women have added stories and elaboration to the Bible over the time before Jesus and since that time. Some stories have been shown conclusively to be fraudulent, such as the Gnostic Gospels; those have been excluded from any consideration at all. Others such as the *Mishnah* (oral traditions of the Jewish teachers said to extend back to Moses on Mount Sinai) have been considered with respect and discernment. Similarly, the thoughts of Christian teachers on origins have been read judiciously, remembering that even Job spoke without knowledge; and furthermore, we are all prone to support our biased ideas about these matters.

Scriptures given are from the King James Version (KJV), unless otherwise specified. Some passages are from The New International Version (NIV), The Orthodox Jewish Bible, The Geneva Bible, and Wycliffe Bible.

Chapter 1

Genesis 1:1 and 1:2

1a. Beginning

The first Hebrew **word** of the Torah or the Pentateuch (five books of Moses) is *bereshit* meaning beginnings (Kaminsky and Lohr 2011). *Bereshis* is the Hebrew name for Genesis, the first book of the *Tanakh* or the Old Testament. Genesis describes a transcendent Creator and the creation of the universe. It describes the beginning of the nation of Israel. It has rightly been called a book of beginnings.

Bereshis 1:1 in Hebrew (right to left) is: אֵת, אֱלֹהִים בָּרָא, בְּרֵאשִׁית
הָאָרֶץ וְאֵת, הַשָּׁמַיִם.

This translates into English literally (left to right): *beginning created God the (alpha & omega) heaven(s) and earth.* The two Hebrew letters in the middle of these seven words are אֵת, aleph and tov, the first and the last of the Hebrew alphabet. The God who created all things is the Alpha and Omega.

Genesis 1:1 is not a summary statement. There are five major reasons for that:

1) the grammatical structure of verse two prohibits it,

2) verse one is declarative followed by "ands" for the work of all six days,

3) God's purposes were established before the beginning,

4) if it is a summary, then there cannot be two heavens, one created first and then one created on day two by separating the waters to make it, and

5) God starts counting with the number one. Each of the five reasons is elaborated upon here.

1. The "waw" or *and* that starts verse two is conjunctive. It continues the main thought expressed in verse one. It begins a dependent clause, describing the condition of the earth after it was created. There are many references one could cite that have argued this including those in Chapter 4 of Weston Fields' book *Unformed and Unfilled* (1976) (also cf. p. 121, Whitcomb 1972). The first two verses essentially say, as I paraphrase, **in the beginning or at the start, God created the heavens and the earth. Now as for the earth, it was not yet completed. It was not filled with everything yet.**

   Even if we might think this "waw" means *afterwards,* as suggested by J. August Dathe in 1789 (p. 15, cited and translated by Custance 1970), it still can be argued afterwards is after the events of the first verse; and not after some hypothesized events occurring between the two verses. It should be noted that Dathe interpreted Genesis 1:1 as a summary statement, not an introductory statement; but Dathe's **afterward** was after some undetermined time and after what he says some remarkable changes had occurred. In other words, Dathe believed in a gap. The gap theories will be discussed at length in later chapters.

2. Genesis 1:1 as an introductory sentence agrees with the view of Karl Keil and Franz Delitzsch (p. 46, 1866, translated from German by J Martin 1949). They said, "This sentence...is not a mere heading, nor a summary of history of the creation, but a declaration of the primeval act of God, by which the universe was called into being." These Lutheran professors also pointed out that all the "*and*s" that follow in Genesis 1 (what they called "different acts of creation") connect to verse one, e.g., Genesis 1:3 "*And* God said..." Genesis 1:5 "*And* God called the light...," Genesis 1:6 "*And* God said..." and so forth.

   John Sailhamer, though a proponent of a gap between Genesis 1:1 and 1:2 similar to Gorman Gray's (see section

4b), tells us that Genesis does not begin with the law or the promises, neither with the natural world or nature, but with creation *ex nihilo*. God starts with nothing, and it is His will to create in order to bestow His goodness upon His creation.

Sailhamer (p. 32, 2009) writes, **"All God's acts recorded in the Pentateuch are grounded in the "real world (biblical realism). Also, the Pentateuch begins with the free action of God in creation... also moves quickly to tell us that the free act was also for our 'good.'"**

3. A verse in Ephesians 3 suggests that the creation of the world was at the very beginning of everything. So too a verse in Revelations 13 helps us grasp that the foundation of the earth occurred at the beginning after it had been predetermined by the Godhead that Jesus Christ would be sacrificed for our sins.

Ephesians 3:9 says, And to make all men see what is the fellowship of the mystery, which from the beginning of the world hath been hid in God, who created all things by Jesus Christ.

Revelation 13:8 says, And all that dwell upon the earth shall worship Him, whose names are not written in the book of life of the Lamb slain from the foundation of the world.

4. If Genesis 1:1 is a summary statement, then the heavens spoken of must be the material heavens—the sky and outer space described as being made on day two. If only material things are being considered here, then nothing spiritual that was made would be listed as being made in days 1-6. But we know from many scriptures that God made everything, including angels and thrones, visible and invisible things. Other scriptures imply that He made angels and everything else in six days. The letter to the Colossians tells us that everything in heaven; e.g., thrones and powers; and on

earth, was made by God. And we read in Exodus 20:11 that in six days the Lord made heaven and earth.

Colossians 1:16 says, For by Him were all things created, that are in heaven, and that are in earth, visible and invisible, whether they be thrones, or dominions, or principalities, or powers: all things were created by Him, and for Him:

This argument was made by St. Augustine in 415 A.D. (p. 27). Augustine contrasted and distinguished what he called **"a spiritual created work already formed and perfected... the heaven [above all]"** that He created as indicated in Genesis 1:1, with the firmament which He made on the second day—this firmament was also called heaven. It was called heaven because of its similarity but the heaven created on the first day was spiritual, and the heaven created on the second day was material.

5. In Genesis 1:1 and 1:2 God begins to count. He counts day one first. But we cannot count first, second, third, until there is a transition to day two. So He calls this day one, and then describes an evening and a morning which is a transition. It is the first transition. As pointed out by Jonathan Sarfati (2003) in referring to a study by Prof. Andrew Steinmann, day one is not called the first day. It is called day one. Light appeared on day one, then there was an evening day-to-night transition and a morning night-to-day transition. Then we have day two or a second day; and when the work is done on day two, we have a second day and a second day transition.

As pointed out by Brock Lee (p. 37, 2009), **"The numbering of the days is consistent with a single week... The numbers make it clear that there is a steady progression or order of days."** Incidentally, this is in the section of Brock Lee's book where he discredits the gap theory. Brock Lee also notes that every verse after the first day, after the second day, and so forth, begins with the word **and**. This validates the concept of a single week of progressive work by God.

A historical report typically provides a chronology. Keil and Delitzsch (1866, translated by J Martin 1949) said, **"The account of creation, its commencement, progress, and completion, bears the marks, both in form and substance of a historical document..."** They also said, **"...its place at the beginning of the book of Genesis is sufficient to warrant the expectation that it will tell us history..."**

Numbers and counting appear to be an organizing component of Genesis 1. The idea of counting is consistent with the Hebrew rabbis who suggest God created 10 things on day one. Rabbi Louis Ginzberg (p. 11, 2008) said God created heaven and earth and *tohu* and *bohu* and light and dark and wind and water and duration of day and duration of night on the first day. The book of *Jubilees* (100 B.C. or 2011) says seven things were created on day one: 1) heavens, 2) earth and water, 3) angels, 4) seasons, 5) abyss and darkness, 6) night and 7) day.

To digress for a moment before we continue to discuss counting day one, second day, and so on; a comment is needed about the concept of zero. Arguments about "*ex nihilo*" not being a concept until the influence of Persian Zoroastrianism, which will be discussed more later (section 5c), is irrelevant for considering whether creation from nothing is implied in Genesis 1:1-2. When counting begins, we do not start with **zero**, we start to count: one. Because counting does not start with zero does not imply there is something there before one, it implies when something is counted the first time, it is number one. When something else is counted, it is number two. The origin of the concept of a zero will be discussed later in regards to the gap theories.

Rabbi Ginzberg is known as a 20th century Talmudist; he came to New York City from Lithuania. He (p. 11, 2008) said "heaven and earth" were made of different elements, but was one unit. The idea of heaven and earth being one unit will be examined in section 1c. Ginzberg said, **"The heavens were fashioned from the light of God's garment; and the earth from the snow under**

the Divine Throne." This is an elaboration from a religious teacher to help with understanding the light and earth that God created. It does not come from canonized scripture, but we respect and read with discernment the Jewish commentators as we do Christian commentators. Ginzberg also explains tradition has it that *tohu* is a green band that disperses darkness. (I would point out this implies something that is able to reflect light, i.e., reflect the green color wavelength, which is the predominant wavelength humans and animals will be able to see once they are created.) *Bohu* are supposed to be stones that produce water.

Being a Talmudist means Ginzberg is trained to use the *Jerusalem Talmud* (400 A.D.) and the *Talmud of Babylonia* (600 A.D.) to render decisions and interpret passages in the Torah and the Mishnah (oral traditions).

In *Legends of the Jews*, the book written by Ginzberg, there is also a description of seven heavens created (p. 12, 2008). Undoubtedly, we should now use thoughtfulness in understanding these legends. Seven heavens are **not** enumerated in the Bible. John Gill (2c, B3, C1, 1767) said these Jewish heavens were mere fables, which is a conclusive opinion to be sure. Nevertheless, is there some wisdom to be gained in considering seven aspects of what could be designated as heaven? Most Christians believe there are three heavens – atmosphere, outer space, and spiritual heaven. Gill (s.2a, B3, C1, 1767) designated the three heavens as the habitation of God's glory, starry heavens, and aerial heavens. Henry Morris (p. 58, 1976) designated them atmospheric, sidereal, and the heaven of God's throne. The seven legendary heavens of the Jews include

1) the atmosphere,

2) outer space,

3) the place of manna,

4) the fourth heaven is celestial Jerusalem with the temple and the angel Michael,

5) the fifth houses angels that praise God,

6) the sixth houses the trials to come upon the earth, and

7) the seventh the Divine Throne surrounded by seraphim and other special angels. There will be more about this in section 1b on heavens.

It is interesting that Ginzberg (p. 8, 2008, also cf. p. 14 Fields 1976) also writes that it is believed 2000 years before the beginning, the Torah {The Law} was created, as well as hell, paradise, the celestial altar, the voice crying out, and the Divine Throne. The Messiah's name is written on the altar, and He is appointed to bring salvation. There seem to be no angels there, just the Godhead and the predetermined plans. This idea is consistent with Scriptures that speak of the Messiah or Lamb of God crucified before the foundation of the earth.

I Peter 1:18-20 says, Forasmuch as ye know that ye were not redeemed with corruptible things, as silver and gold, from your vain conversation received by tradition from your fathers; But with the precious blood of Christ, as of a lamb without blemish and without spot: Who verily was foreordained before the foundation of the world, but was manifest in these last times for you.

The Midrash Tehillim, Part II states that seven things were created two thousand years before creation (Braude, p. 94). Rabbi Zeira (3rd century) taught that repentance is great because it was created before the world. Psalm 90:3 says "Repent, ye children of men." Psalm 90:4 says "For a thousand years in Thy sight are but as yesterday when it is past." Combining these two passages with Proverbs 8:30, "Then I was with Him, as a nursling; and I was day by day His delight," allowed Rabbi Lakish (2nd century) to arrive at there being two days each being 1,000 years in which wisdom was God's delight. Rabbi Sholom Schneerson (1892-1920, transl. E Touger) wrote 2,000 years does not designate time because before creation there was no time. He said the Hebrew word *aleph* for thousand sounds like *aelefcha* for I will teach you. Two stands for: I will teach you wisdom, I will teach you understanding.

Let us continue our discussion of counting one, two, three … The first Hebrew letter of the Bible is *bait*, the second letter of the

Hebrew alphabet. It resembles a house set on the ground with a dot in the middle representing one who lives there (p. 12, Kushner 1975). Lawrence Kushner explains there are two little points on the upper left of the letter. One little point points to He who made the letter (it points above), and the other little point points to the first letter *alef*, as if to say, "He came before" and "One is His name."

Another tradition held by the Jews is that *bait* begins the Torah {Pentateuch} because it is only open to the left, in the direction one reads, designating that we should "concern ourselves with the day the world was created and onward. Here and now!" (p. 14, Kushner 1975). This idea is consistent with Genesis 1:1 beginning the counting of days. It is also consistent with God being the only **One** present before creation began. The Jewish tradition about the first letter *aleph* is covered in the next section on heavens.

The idea of what was created in the beginning is symbolized by the house with someone in it. *Bait* means a house, and *bait* is the number two. The house is both heaven and earth created by God as a dwelling place. In fact, there are two houses: one for God – heaven, and one for man – the cosmos. Heaven is a place for God to dwell in His administration of love and goodness to man. Earth is a place for man to dwell, and to commune with God, and to be at home.

Psalm 114:16 says, The heaven, even the heavens, are the Lord's: but the earth hath He given to the children of men.

One other point must be made here about the beginning. In Luke 11 we have a scripture that speaks of the beginning (NIV) as being "from the blood of Abel that was shed." The King James Version of this same verse is translated "from the foundation of the world." It would seem that beginning can be used to refer to the six days of creation, or to the beginning of the family of man. It is the beginning of a number of things. It also would seem that "foundation of the world" can refer to the six days of creation, or to the beginning of the family of man. We will return to the foundation of the earth in discussing when angels were created in section 1d.

1b. Heavens

This brings us to our next topic. What are heavens or heaven, the Hebrew words *HaShomayim* and *Shomayim*? In Hebrew, *shomayim* is distinguished from *eretz* (earth) and *sheol* (underworld).

Bereshis 1:1 (*Orthodox Jewish Bible*) says, In the beginning Elohim created hashomayim and haaretz.

In Devarim 10:14 (Deuteronomy) (*Orthodox Jewish Bible*) it says, Behold, the Shomayim and Shomei HaShomayim (highest heaven) belong to Hashem Eloheidia...

In Bereshis 1:8 we read, And Elohim called the raki'a Shomayim (Heaven).

In this case, it is heaven without the *ha*. The ha as a prefix added to *shomayim* to make it *Hashomayim* would seem to make it The Heavens. It could be said that the *raki'a* is the sky or the gate of heaven (simply *shomayim*).

There are no singular or plural tenses in Hebrew for these two nebulous formless, relatively invisible substances. There is no plural or singular for this word *shomayim* (heaven) in Hebrew. Also there is no plural for *mayim* (water).

Since there is no singular or plural for *mayim*, it means water or waters. Note that *shomayim* and *mayim* refer to somewhat invisible substances, air and water respectively, and we should say perhaps in the case of *hashomayim* a completely invisible realm of the spiritual heaven.

Bereshis 1:6 (*Orthodox Jewish Bible*) says, And Elohim said, let there be a raki'a in the midst of the mayim (waters), and let it divide the mayim from the mayim.

When we recognize the debate amongst ancient rabbis in the Talmud as allowing for more than one answer by different rabbis (perhaps conflicting answers), we can choose to agree or disagree with each individual answer. We don't have to accept the whole teaching to accept portions of it (pp. 46-47, Rosen and Rosen 1976). Isn't meditating on scripture doing the same thing? There is a certain logic and consistency associated with different possible answers to a question.

The Talmudic masters discussed the words of Genesis 1:1 (p. 4, Finkel 2004). They ask, **What is the origin of the word** *shamayim*, **"heaven"? R. Yose b. R. Chanina said: It is a contraction of** *sham mayim*, **"there is water in that place." Alternatively, it was taught:** *Shamayim* **is a combination of** *esh* **and** *mayim*, **"fire and water." This teaches us that God brought fire and water together and mixed them, making the sky out of them (Chagigah 12a).**

We can see truth in both of these comments. God hovered over the waters suggests that initially the heaven itself had water in it or water was a barrier between heaven and earth. Secondly, if light or fire interacted with water, we know chemically the hydrogen and oxygen of H_2O can be separated out, and produce oxygen and hydrogen of the atmosphere.

In the book, *A Rabbinical Commentary on Genesis* (1949, translated from Polish by PI Hershon), the rabbi discusses why the Torah {Pentateuch} begins with second letter *beth*, and also why the first book is not just a listings of precepts or laws. The sages (p. 2, Ashkenazi 1949) say the world was created by God for

1) the Torah {The Law},

2) the temple, and

3) the tithes or first-fruits.

The Temple was created before the world (not way before, but perhaps just before on day one). This is consistent with spiritual heavens on day one and earth on day three, as described in Genesis 1. In the beginning, God created the heaven and the earth. At the creation of heaven and earth, the earth was desolate and void, it was incomplete; and God's throne of glory hovered in the air over the water, said Rabbi Ashkenazi.

In the New Testament, we see that God's throne or His tabernacle is equated with heaven. God Himself cannot be entirely contained in any heaven, but a heavenly tabernacle was **made for**

God by God, as explained in Hebrews 8:2. God the Father and God the Son are in this heaven with the Son awaiting all things to be accomplished as foretold as He sits at the right hand of the Father.

Matthew 5:34 says, But I say unto you, Swear not at all; neither by heaven; for it is God's throne:

Hebrews 8:2 says, A minister [Jesus Christ] of the sanctuary, and of the true tabernacle, which the Lord pitched, and not man.

Acts 2:35 says, The Lord said to my Lord: Sit at my right hand until I make your enemies a footstool for your feet.

Ginzberg (pp. 9-11, 2008), as well as Kushner (p. 9, 1975), explain that the first book of the Torah begins with the letter *beth* because it is the first letter of the word "beginning" and the word "blessings." *Aleph*, the first letter, complained that *beth* was the second letter of the alphabet, and she *Aleph* should begin the book. God explained that *aleph* is the first letter of the 10 Commandments (Decalogue) given on Mount Sinai. The Decalogue begins, **I am the Lord thy God**; the word "I" begins with the letter *aleph*.

The Decalogue or Ten Commandments is the essence of God's way, or the Way. As Christians we understand that the Torah {The Law} is the schoolteacher leading to fulfillment of the Law in the Messiah.

Galatians 3:24 says, Wherefore the law was our schoolmaster to bring us unto Christ, that we might be justified by faith.

Jesus calls Himself the Way (John 14:6); Jesus calls Himself the Alpha, the First, as recorded in Revelation. He is *aleph* as well as the fulfillment (*tov*). God is called the first and the last in the Old Testament too.

In Isaiah 48:12-13 God says …I am He; I am the first and the last. My own hand laid the foundations of the earth, and my right hand spread out the heavens; when I summon them, they all stand together.

A Rabbinical Commentary on Genesis (p. 6, Ashkenazai 1885) says that light was created on the first day, but it was not suspended in heaven until the fourth day. There are many other sources discussing the light of the first day, that it was not the sun—Jewish sources describing it as spiritual light (the light of Torah); Messianic Jews describing it as the Messianic light; Christian sources saying it was the light of God which will be the source of light in the new Jerusalem as explained in the book of Revelation. We will come back to this issue of light on the first day versus the light of the sun created on the fourth day. As for the idea that the Lord Jesus as highly exalted, and is the Light, let's look at Revelation.

Revelation 21:23 says And the city had no need of the sun, neither of the moon, to shine on it; for the glory of God did lighten it, and the Lamb is the light thereof.

Revelation 22:5 says, And there shall be no night there, and they have no need of candle, neither light of the sun; for the Lord God giveth them light. And they shall reign forever and ever.

A little more can be said about the light that was spoken into existence in the earthly realm on day one. The Talmud (p. 5, Finkel 2004) says, **The Sages explain the luminaries were created on the first day, but they were not hung up in the sky until the fourth day (Chagigah 12a).**

This is not such a different view than the creating-and-making account of Delmar Dobberpuhl (p. 79, 2011), who proposes that the sun, moon, and stars were partially created on the second and third day as proto-stars, proto-moons, and so forth. These lights were clumps of matter made from the waters above created on the first day; they would not have been visible on earth until day four, according to Dobberpuhl who is a retired physicist.

The light from God was spoken into the darkness of some sort of "formlessness" or "formless substance." This was the first light to appear in the material realm, and it could only have come from God who dwells in the absolute incomprehensible unapproachable Light. The light given from God was the means by which all things were created. We read about it in Colossians.

Colossians 1:15 says, Who is the image of the invisible God, the firstborn of every creature:

This verse from Colossians **does say** that Jesus is the image of the Father, but it **does not say** that He had a beginning – rather, it says that He is the light and life of everything created. This is acknowledged by the apostle John at the beginning of his gospel. Jesus is with God and is God, and He is the Light allowing everything to be created. Furthermore, John states that the Word is the Life of all men.

John 1:1-5 says, In the beginning was the Word, and the Word was with God, and the Word was God. The same was in the beginning with God. All things were made by Him; and without Him was not any thing made that was made. In Him was life; and the life was the light of men. And the light shineth in darkness; and the darkness comprehended it not.

I digress here to mention the Aramaic word **Memra** (Word) of God is found in the *Targumim* (p. 547, Boyarin 2010). The *Targumim* are explanations of the Jewish scriptures written in Aramaic. David Boyarin, professor of Talmudic Culture at UC, Berkeley, explains the idea of Memra (translated Logos in Greek) has been controversial in Judaism, with some rabbis objecting to there being two powers in heaven. But the *Targum Neofiti* explains that God tells Moses at the burning bush to go to Pharaoh and, "I, My Memra, will be with you." It is also instructive to see what the Targumic poetic homily on the "Four Nights" says. Boyarin quotes, **"Four nights are written in the Book of Memories: The first night: when the Lord was revealed above the world to create it. The world was unformed and void and darkness was spread over the surface of the deep; and through His Memra there was light and illumination, and He called it the first night."**

I see a connection between the Holy Spirit, the Word, and God in the Old and New Testaments.

Genesis 1:2 tells us the Spirit of God hovered over the waters.

Philippians 1:19 identifies the Holy Spirit as the Spirit of Jesus Christ.

In Matthew 3:16 the Spirit of God descends like a dove on Jesus after He is baptized by John the Baptist.

Boyarin (p. 547, 2002) writes of Philo of Alexandria incorporating the Word of God (Logos) with the Wisdom of God (Sophia) as all part of the godhead.

Isaiah 11:2-3 reveals that wisdom is an integral aspect of the Holy Spirit. It is paradoxically difficult to separate the Father, Son, and Holy Ghost of the Trinity, who is the One and Only True God.

Isaiah 11:2-3 (NIV) says, The Spirit of the Lord will rest on him— the Spirit of wisdom and of understanding, the Spirit of counsel and of might, the Spirit of the knowledge and fear of the Lord— and he will delight in the fear of the Lord.

The Lord is the Light, and the light given comes from Him. So too in the new heavens and new earth, He will be the Light. We know as scientists that light always emanates from its source in some direct or indirect way. So we can call the source of light "the light." It also tells us in scripture that God is the Father of Lights – the plural here indicates more than one light. We read in the *Orthodox Jewish Bible* that every good and complete gift comes from the Father of Lights who has no variation. We remember God gives light. He created light. He placed the greater and lesser lights and the stars in the heavens for us. To debate about whether He is the light or He gives the light is only important in the context in which the word light is used. He also made angels who shine forth with heavenly light. God is the Father of many lights.

We will discuss more about the creation of angels below. I will add here that this rabbinical commentary also says (p. 8, Ashkenazai 1885), **"He [God] alone made him on earth as He alone made the angels in heaven; alike in understanding and similitude."** This implies that both men and angels were created by God to have a spiritual nature. This would also suggest that angels and man were both created during the first week, in the beginning – angels on the first day inhabiting heaven, and man on the sixth day, completing the creation of earth. This of course would include the angel who would become the enemy or Satan, and those fallen angels that rebelled with him.

Furthermore, in Psalm 33 we read that God created the angels by the breath of His mouth. In Genesis we are told that man became a living soul when God breathed into him. So the spirit of angels and man were both created by the breath of God. Both angels and man were created with an immortal soul to live forever.

Psalm 33:6 (Tehilim 33:6, *Orthodox Jewish Bible*) says, By the Devar (word) Hashem (Lord) were Shomayim (heavens) made; and all the tz'va (host) of them by the ruach (breath) of His mouth.

Genesis 2:7 says, He breathed into man's nostrils and man became a living soul.

Regarding when Satan was created and who he was, Jesus said something about that to the Jews who claimed Abraham as their father, as recorded in John.

John 8:44, Ye are of your father the devil... He was a murderer from the beginning, and abode not in the truth, because there is no truth in him...

It would seem that the devil himself was deceitful and evil as soon as he was able to make a choice to either follow God or his own derisive desires; i.e., as soon as he was created along with the other angels at the very beginning. This idea was suggested by Boston College professor Peter Kreeft (p. 93, 1995) who stated, **"At the moment of their creation they [angels] choose for or against God forever. They cannot change their fundamental choice."**

Another scripture mentioning murder and beginning is found in the book of Luke.

Luke 11:50 says, Therefore this generation will be held responsible for the blood of all the prophets that has been shed since the beginning of the world.

This scripture tells us that Cain, the first man ever born to Adam and Eve, was alive at the beginning of human history. So it would seem that pertaining to mankind the word "beginning" indicates early in human history, when Adam and Eve were created and had sons Cain and Abel, as man began to multiply on the earth. Here Jesus accuses these particular Pharisees of being like those who slayed the prophets of God including Cain who slayed Abel. These Pharisees were like Satan who was a murderer.

A passage in I John says that Cain belonged to the evil (or wicked) one.

Luke 11:50-51 says, That the blood of all the prophets, which was shed from the foundation of the world, may be required of this generation, from the blood of Abel unto the blood of Zacharias...

I John 3:12 says, ... Cain, who was of that wicked one, and slew his brother.

So when was Satan created and when did he fall? I will return to the creation of angels in general later, but pertaining to the beginning, we also have the translated word "ancient."

In Revelation 9:9 The great dragon was hurled down – that **ancient** serpent called the devil, or Satan, who leads the whole world astray.

Ancient is used to refer to very distance past events like in I Samuel 27:8 an ancient people, I Chronicles 4:22 to ancient records, and I Peter 2:5 referring to the ancient world (referring to the pre-flood world). Ancient in these passages does not mean billions of years; it means very far in the past.

Further scriptures help us discern when Satan was created. Undoubtedly, he was created with the other angels.

I John 3:8 says, He that committeth sin is of the devil; for the devil sinneth from the beginning.

In Isaiah 14:12, Satan is called the morning star and son of the dawn. This implies that he was created at the beginning. When did he sin? This would be as soon as his will was tested, suggested by John 8:44 and I John 3:8 (see above) to be at the beginning. It is written that Satan was created perfect until wickedness was found in him (Ezekiel 28:15). He is the tempter; and just as man is tempted when he is drawn away from obedience to God, and enticed, so Satan was disobedient to God. He fell at the beginning. Satan had a plan to tempt Adam and Eve, and he carried it out quickly.

1c. Heaven and Earth

So if heaven and earth is one unit, as stated by Rabbi Ginzberg, then we should talk about the creation of them together.

So what does the phrase *"hashomayim and haaretz"* (Bereshis 2:2) really mean? The Jewish legend would have it be: one unit created together, complete within itself. It is the heavenly heavens plus the substance that would become shaped into (or plus the space into which would be put) sky, land, sea, outer space, solar systems, stars, and galaxies, plants, animals, and man. (As you can deduce, I am not committed entirely to

#1 - God creating a type of material that was made into other things, or

#2 - God creating each individual thing; but it was all supernaturally done in the first six days.

I tend to favor #2.) The scripture does tell us God said let the earth bring forth the living creatures, and the water teemed with living creatures. God created them all supernaturally. In the *Wycliffe Bible*, we read in Genesis 1:20-21 both "waters bring forth" and "made of nought" as translations of what happened when God commanded creatures to be in the seas and birds in the air on the fifth day.

Genesis 1:20-21a (*Wycliffe Bible*) says, Also God said (And God said), The **waters bring forth** a reptile, either a creeping beast, of living soul, and a volatile, either a bird flying above [the] earth, under the firmament of (the) heaven(s). And God **made of nought** great whales, and each living soul and movable, which the waters have brought forth in their kinds; and God made of nought each volatile by his kind.

These two things: heaven and earth were created first. After this unit was created, the *haaretz* was dark; and then on this first day God spoke light into existence. Light or electromagnetic energy would be needed to make the material universe. It would seem that the earth in verse 2 would be an empty space ready to be filled.

But before we discuss physical light that was probably needed to create other things, let us further consider what God created in Genesis 1:1.

Passages found in both Isaiah and Acts corroborate that God created the heavenly heaven and the material world. The throne of God would be in the spiritual heavens.

Isaiah 66:1 says, Thus saith the Lord, The heaven is my throne, and the earth is my footstool; where is the house that he build unto me?

Acts 7:49 says, Heaven is my throne, and earth is my footstool; what house will ye build me?

So where does God really dwell?

The Bible tells us that God dwells in unapproachable Light.

The sages (p. 2, Ashkenazi 1949) say that the earth being desolate and void meant that the Shekinah was not present. They also said this signifies the departing of the Shekinah when the temple would be destroyed in the future.

Custance (p. 31, 1957) stated, **"It is also of interest to note that Gen. 1.2 was interpreted as a global condition resulting from the withdrawal of the Shekinah glory."**

Finkel (pp. 20-21, 1996) said, **"Kabbalah teaches that at the beginning of Creation, God's Infinite Light filled all of reality. Within this Divine Light nothing else could exist. Therefore, before bringing the universe into being, God made 'room' for it by yielding space, in a process called *tzimtzum,* which means stricture, or contraction of His Infinite Light. To put it another way, God withdrew into Himself, leaving a vast primordial void in the middle of His Infinity."**

There are a number of scripture verses describing God dwelling in unapproachable light. Also the Bible tells us that no man can see God and live. There are also scriptures saying that God does not dwell in temples.

Daniel 2:22 records that Daniel said, He revealeth the deep and secret things: He knoweth what is in the darkness, and the light dwelled with Him.

In I Timothy 6:16 it speaks of Jesus Christ, King of Kings as He, Who only has immortality, dwelling in the light which no man can approach unto; whom no man hath seen, nor can see: to whom be honour and power everlasting. Amen.

I John 1:5 says that God is light, and in Him is no darkness at all.

James 1:7 says, Every good gift and every perfect gift is from above, and cometh down from the Father of lights, with Whom is no variableness, neither shadow of turning.

John 6:46, Not that any man hath seen the Father, save He which is of God, He hath seen the Father.

John 1:18 No man hath seen God at any time; the only begotten son, which is in the bosom of the Father, He hath declared Him.

As for scripture related to seeing God and dying,

Exodus 33:20 says, And He said, Thou canst not see my face: for there shall no man see me, and live.

But of course, there are persons who saw the angel of the Lord and lived, including Moses, Jacob, the parents of Samuel before he was born, Elijah, Joshua, Isaiah, and others. These persons did not see God the Father in unapproachable light. They saw Him who is called the angel of the Lord. Many Bible Scholars believe this Angel is the preincarnate Jesus.

Lastly, scriptures related to God not dwelling in an earthly tabernacle or temples are in both the Old and New Testaments.

I King 8:27 (and II Chronicles 6:18 is similar), But will God indeed dwell on the earth? Behold, the heaven, and heaven of heavens cannot contain thee; how much less this house that I have builded?

Acts 7:28, Howbeit the most High dwelleth not in temples made by hands, as saith the prophet.

One more point to be made is that "swearing by heaven and earth" is presumably not swearing by the planet earth and outer space. When Abraham sent his servant to get a wife for Isaac, he had his servant swear by "the Lord, the God of heaven, and the God of the earth…" (Genesis 24:3). If God is just the God of the universe and not heaven too, then He would not be as great as if He is God of the spiritual heaven too.

God is the creator of the spiritual heavens and the material universe, presumably designated as heaven and earth. We see this in the Old Testament. In the New Testament, there is a verse where Jesus identifies God as Lord of heaven and earth. In this case too, the heaven spoken of is customarily interpreted as the spiritual heaven.

Genesis 14:19 says, And He blessed him, and said, Blessed be Abram of the most high God, possessor of heaven and earth:

(Genesis 14:19 in the NIV says. creator of heaven and earth).

Luke 10:21 says, In that hour Jesus rejoiced in spirit, and said, I thank thee, O Father, Lord of heaven and earth,

So the heaven spoken of in Genesis 1:1 is most assuredly spiritual heaven. So we might ask, where was God before the spiritual heavens? Wasn't He always abiding in heaven? The answer would seem to be no; not in the spiritual heaven that was created in the beginning. He dwells in unapproachable light, and before **anything** was created, He was everything and everywhere. Everything that He created is less than Him. He had to fashion a space for that which would be less than Him. As mentioned above, He removed Himself from a space where He would create everything visible and invisible, spiritual and material. Even the spiritual heavens are less than God Himself, the Godhead Himself Themselves.

Thus, we now ask, why did He suddenly decide to create heaven and earth? The commentators, both Jewish and Christian, answer in various ways: He wanted to express His love; or He as a King choose to create a kingdom where He could express His love. Some theologians emphasize that it was His will to create. We know from John 1:1 that the Word was with God and was God in the beginning; and without a doubt the Godhead (which we believe are Father, Son, and Holy Ghost) all existed before the beginning, from everlasting to everlasting! It makes sense that God created heaven and earth, set up His rule of government, and created angels to worship Him as well as teach mankind how to worship Him. Angels were created to minister to mankind; they reveal prophetic insight, they protect from harm, they help provide for man's needs, and they rejoice with us His people.

Psalm 148:2 says, Praise Him, all His angels, all the armies of heaven.

Psalm 103:20 says, Bless the Lord, ye His angels; that excel in strength, that do His commandments, hearkening unto the voice of His word.

Hebrews 1:7 says, And of the angels He saith, Who maketh His angels spirits, and His ministers a flame of fire.

Two passages from the book of Isaiah also indicate that Jesus is the first and the last. If Jesus is the first, He reigns as King from the very beginning. If He is the last, the purposes of God are accomplished in Him and for Him.

Isaiah 44:6 says, Thus saith the LORD the King of Israel, and His redeemer the LORD of hosts; I am the first, and I am the last; and beside me there is no God.

Isaiah 48:12 says, Hearken unto me, O Jacob and Israel, my called; I am He; I am the first, I also am the last.

My case for everything, including heaven, angels, and the cosmos (the earth with its universe) being created in six days is based on two primary truths.

The first is that Jesus is the Alpha and Omega.

The second is the concept of beginning being the "very beginning" of everything created. It follows that there would be no gap neither between Genesis 1:1 and 1:2, nor before Genesis 1:1. Another scripture tells us that everything was created in six days; some might take this as being everything material, but the case is made here that this is everything, spiritual and material.

Exodus 20:11 says, For in six days the Lord made heaven and earth, the sea, and all that in them is, and rested the seventh day: wherefore the Lord blessed the sabbath day, and hallowed it.

With so many scriptures telling us that God is the creator of all things, and in many cases: e.g., in Nehemiah, we are told that He created earth, heaven, and **angels**. It makes sense that these were all created at the beginning. In addition, Psalm 104 includes God created earth and **angels** in the same passage.

Nehemiah 9:6 Thou, even thou, art Lord alone; thou hast made heaven and the heaven of heavens, with all their host, the earth, and all things that are therein, and thou preservest them all; and the host of heaven worshippeth thee.

Psalm 104:1-6 says,

Bless the Lord, O my soul. O Lord my God, thou art very great; Thou art clothed with honour and majesty. Who coverest thyself with light as with a garment: who stretchest out the heavens like a curtain: Who layeth the beams of His chambers in the waters: who maketh the clouds His chariot: who walketh upon the wings of the wind: Who maketh His angels spirits; His ministers a flaming fire: Who laid the foundations of the earth, that it should not be removed for ever. Thou coveredst it with the deep as with a garment: the waters stood above the mountains.

These verses include God hiding Himself, or covering Himself with light. If God dwells in Divine Light, and the created things are separate from that Light, then He is covering Himself up or preventing the fullness of the Divine Light of His presence to enter the created order. Another verse speaking of God hiding Himself is found in Isaiah.

Isaiah 45:15 says, Verily thou art a God that hidest thyself, O God of Israel, the Savior.

Psalm 104 describes Him laying the beams of His chambers above the waters, which alludes to the Holy Spirit hovering over the waters. It also declares that angels are spiritual beings and ministers – we might ask, ministers to whom? Angels minister to God and to mankind. Finally, that fact that **all** created beings are under His Rulership is seen too in a passage of scripture from Isaiah 45.

Isaiah 48:12-13 says …I am He; I am the first and the last. My own hand laid the foundations of the earth, and my right hand spread out the heavens; when I summon them, they all stand up together.

See also Isaiah 45:12 …all their host have I commanded.

We also read in Genesis 1:1 the phrase: heaven **and** earth; which could very well indicate that heaven was created before earth, because heaven comes first in the sequence. The heavenly things were created before the earthly things. Then the heavens would have been completed before God began His tasks involving the material substance of the cosmos. He would then proceed to speak light into existence, and bring about day and night and the transition to day two. Furthermore, if the following days would have been the time for creating sky and outer space and heavenly bodies like stars, then the heavens created in verse one would have to be spiritual in nature.

There is another argument that can be made for Genesis 1:1 speaking of creating heavenly heavens and not outer space.

If

1) the firmament is the sky and outer space created on day two and filled with heavenly bodies on day four and birds on day five, and if

2) the first verse of Genesis is not a summary statement, then

3) HEAVENS IN GENESIS 1:1 MUST BE SPIRITUAL HEAVENS.

Psalm 102:25 says, Of old hast thou laid the foundation of the earth: and the heavens are the work of thy hands.

Hebrews 1:10 says, And, Thou, Lord, in the beginning hast laid the foundation of the earth; and the heavens are the works of thine hands:

These two scriptures tell us that in the beginning (of old) both the foundation of the earth and the heavens were created. Referring back to Genesis 1:1 and the first words of the Bible saying, "In the beginning..." This would also imply that the foundations of the earth were established on this first day also.

You might ask how about Psalm 19:1. This passage refers to both heavens and firmament. As you read it notice that the part that can be seen and studied and that displays His handiwork is the firmament; whereas the glory of God is declared by the heavens. The angels and the spiritual revelations come from the spiritual heaven and are declared to us. This scripture has puzzled me. Superficially it seems to convey that the beauty of the galaxies and stars at night and of the clouds and birds during the day tells us about the glory of God. On a deeper level, both the spiritual and material heavens testify to God's unfathomable glory. The angels and spiritual revelations come from the spiritual heaven and are declared to us. Eye has not seen nor ear heard... but God has revealed them to us by His Spirit, says I Corinthians 2:9-10.

Psalm 19:1 says, The heavens declare the glory of God; and the firmament sheweth His handiwork.

A case can be made that spiritual heaven is a place. Objects like a throne, and a right and left side, or seraphim with six wings can be seen there, and this demonstrates that it has dimensions. The throne that Isaiah saw may be prophetic, showing forth a future time when Jesus is Ruler over all with everything put under His feet. It is almost identical to that seen by John in the vision recorded in Revelation, but whether past, present, or future (probably all three), this heaven with a throne is a place.

I King 22:19 says, And he [the prophet Micaiah] said, Hear thou therefore the word of the Lord: I saw the Lord sitting on His throne, and all the host of heaven standing by Him on His right hand and on His left.

Isaiah 6:1 says, In the year that king Uzziah died I saw also the Lord sitting upon a throne, high and lifted up, and His train filled the temple.

Revelations 4:8 says, And the four beasts had each of them six wings about him; and they were full of eyes within: and they rest not day and night, saying, Holy, holy, holy, Lord God Almighty, which was, and is, and is to come.

That a future heaven is a place can also be verified using scripture. Passages from Hebrews and Revelation speak of a city made by God. The future heaven is yet to descend from God to a place on a new earth. The Bible tells us that the present heaven and earth will be rolled up, and a new heaven and earth will be created by God. Jesus said He went to prepare a place for us. This suggests that heaven is a place with length, width, and height. It is not just some imperceptible higher dimension or an ethereal spiritual realm without any dimensions at all.

Isaiah 34:4 says, And all the host of heaven shall be dissolved, and the heavens shall be rolled together as a scroll:

Isaiah 65:17 says, For, behold, I create new heavens and a new earth: and the former shall not be remembered, nor come into mind.

Hebrews 11:10 says, For he [Abraham] looked for a city which hath foundations, whose builder and maker is God.

Hebrews 11:16 says, But now they [Abel, Enoch, Noah, Abraham, Sarah] desire a better country, that is, an heavenly: wherefore God is not ashamed to be called their God: for He hath prepared for them a city.

Revelation 21:15 says, And he [the angel] that talked with me had a golden reed to measure the city, and the gates thereof, and the wall thereof.

Revelation 21:10 says, And he carried me away in the spirit to a great and high mountain, and shewed me that great city, the holy Jerusalem, descending out of heaven from God,

John 14:2 says, In my Father's house are many mansions: if it were not so, I would have told you. I go to prepare a place for you.

The last argument I will make for the heavens of Genesis 1:1 being spiritual is based on the simplicity of God's revealed truths in the Bible. What do we tell our little son or daughter when they ask us, "If God made everything, who made God?"

Our answer, "No one made God; God lives forever and ever."

In reply to, "Where does God live?" we say, "God lives in heaven."

Then, "Where did heaven come from?"

We say, "God made heaven to be His throne, from whence to rule over everything that He created. He created angels to help Him."

Finally, "When did He do that?"

We reply, "The Bible tells us this all happened at the very beginning."

And the child asks, "But wasn't God always there? Where was He before heaven was created?"

Or alternatively if we say, "Heaven was always there," they would reply "Were angels always there?"

We would say, "No, God created angels."

The child responds, "When did God create angels? Was there a time when there were no angels in heaven, just God?"

Stop and think about it. What does the Bible tell us?

1d. Angels

There is no doubt God knows we—both as children or as adults—would ask about angels, and wonder at their significance. We wonder at when they were created. Why does the Bible not tell us explicitly when they were created? Perhaps it does tell us very specifically, but we just have not been childlike enough in faith to see that this is implicit again and again in the scriptures that speak of God creating the heavens.

It seems to me that Psalm 104 refers to the initial creation of heaven and earth all in one psalm. It speaks of God being clothed and covered with light, also that He makes chambers for Himself, He makes angels, and He lays the foundations of the earth. This refers to what He did as reported in Genesis 1:1. It is consistent with the heavens being spiritual and the foundations of the earth being established initially, and being covered with the deep. The King James goes on to say in verse six that the waters stood above the mountains. I know that Gorman Gray uses this verse to provide evidence that God created the whole planet with ground and seas; and Gray thinks even the solar system, and galaxies, as well as the earth were created before the six days. I do not interpret this verse in this manner. I interpret it to be at first the earth was covered with water; then as the ocean basins deepened, the waters flowed down into them to make the seas. God supernaturally created the landscape with mountains and oceans on the third day. The psalm goes on to speak of mountains and seas, animals, and the wonders of the beautiful earth that He created in the six days.

Psalm 104:4 says, Who maketh His angels spirits; His ministers a flaming fire.

Many creationists who accept a young earth accept that angels were created before the foundations of the earth were set in place. Does "this time when the foundations were set in place" refer to

1) day one when the earth was established but was not yet fully formed, or

2) day three, or

3) the whole six days of creation? Some believe it refers to day three when the mountains, the land, and seas were fully formed. Therefore, depending on our view of "this time when the foundations were set in place," most would consent to holding a view that angels were created before day one or before day three, but definitely some time before the six days ended.

In Job 38, we have scriptures referring to the angels (or sons of God) rejoicing as the foundations of the earth were established. I believe the verses of the first half of Job 38 are referring to what happened in the first three days. The second half goes on to describe aspects of the universe and the history of mankind on the earth and animal life on earth, but the first part of the chapter describes the foundations of the earth when the angels sang for joy.

From this we can say the "this time when the foundations were set in place" would be either day one or sometime during days 1-3.

Most young earth creationists agree to some extent with Henry Morris' analysis of when angels were created. In *The Genesis Record* (p. 57, 1976), Henry Morris wrote,

"Although not mentioned in Genesis 1, it is probable that another act of creation took place on this first day. Sometime prior to the third day of creation, a multitude of angels had been created, since they were present when the 'foundations of the earth' were laid – probably a reference to the establishing of solid land surface on the earth."

Dr. Morris also suggested that the angels could not have existed before day one, **"since their sphere of operation in this** universe and their very purpose is to the minister to the 'heirs of salvation' (Hebrews 1:14)."

I believe the Bible teaches that angels were created on day one; Henry Morris thought this was probably the case. Christian Answers Net (affiliated with Films for Christ, which moved from Arizona to Washington) also suggests the same, quoting from Dr. Paul E. Eymann (1996), who taught Bible at *Arizona State University* in Phoenix.

"The time of their creation is never definitely specified, but it is most probably that it occurred in connection with the creation of the heavens in Genesis 1:1. It may be that God created the angels immediately after He had created the heavens and before He created the earth – for according to Job 38:4-7, 'the sons of God shouted for joy' when He laid the foundations of the earth."

Other creationists summarize their thoughts about when angels were created in various books and articles. A worthy example of this reasoning is that of theology professor Douglas Kelly in his *Creation and Change* (pp. 93-94, 1997).

Kelly states, **"Neither Genesis, nor any other text in Scripture states when the angelic beings were actually created. What is definite is that angels are creatures, and thus do have a beginning. ...they may not have been created until the sixth day, when mankind, the primary focus of their activities, was created. ...Perhaps the angels were brought into being on the very first day of creation. ...It has been suggested that since the angels are at times related to the stars...they may have been created on the same day as the luminaries – the fourth. ... passages above from Job 38 and Psalm 104 appear to indicate their presence at least by the third day."**

So if the angels were created during the first six days of creation, they were not present before Genesis 1:1. Perhaps John Wesley was hinting at angels being about 6000 years old when Wesley said in his Sermon No. 77 (cited by Lockyer 1997, p. 38),

"And what an inconceivable degree of wisdom must they [angels] have acquired, by the use of their amazing facilities,

over above that with which they were originally endowed, in the course of six thousand years!"

However, it would seem that many present-day Christian leaders and theologians believe angels were present before Genesis 1:1. In a 2003 Kentucky newspaper advice column, Billy Graham stated, **"The Bible does indicate, however, that the angels were created long before God made the world"** (Q&A 2003). Rev. Billy Graham goes on to talk about the rebellion of Lucifer and the fallen angels occurring before creation. In Graham's 1994 book (p. 68), he expresses that the important question is not when the angels were created or when Satan and his angels fell, but rather to know that they were created and that they did fall. He said the question of **when** "must remain unanswered."

Professor Dickason (p. 142, 1995) of *Moody Bible Institute* was of the opinion that angels could have been created either in Genesis 1:1 or before that because they rejoiced when the foundations of the earth were made. Dickason said, **"If we assume that angels were part of the creation of Genesis 1:1, then their fall follows that point. However, it may be that angels were created prior to the creation of the heavens and the earth."**

Most students of the Bible do not think a lot about angels. We sometimes assume God has always had angels worshipping Him. But the Bible clearly teaches that angels were created.

Psalm 108:2, 5 says, Praise Him, all His angels, Praise Him, all His heavenly hosts... for He commanded and they were created.

Perhaps we recall the passage in Revelation where angels are worshipping the Lamb.

Revelation 5: 11-12 says, And I beheld, and I heard the voice of many angels round about the throne and the beasts and the elders: and the number of them was ten thousand times ten thousand, and thousands of thousands; saying with a loud voice, Worthy is the Lamb that was slain to receive power, and riches, and wisdom, and strength, and honour, and glory, and blessing.

The argument that these angels in this passage were worshipping God at the redemption of the "whole created order" was made by Doug Kelly (p. 93, Kelly 1997). The fact that we see the angels worshipping the Lamb who had redeemed the believers in Revelation does not necessarily imply that angels were worshipping God for all eternity past or even any time prior to Genesis 1:1. If we accept that Genesis 1:1 refers to the spiritual heavens being created on day one, then it follows that the angels could have been created at that time too.

One of the duties of angels is to show man how to worship God. They themselves are not to be worshipped. They invariably instruct persons that are in awe of their glory not to bow down to them. An example of this is seen in Revelation.

Revelation 22:9 says, Then saith he [the angel] unto me, see thou do it not [bow down to me]: for I am thy fellow servant, and of thy brethren the prophets, and of them which keep the sayings of this book, worship God.

Peter Kreeft (p. 93, 1995), put forth the view that angels are in spiritual time and do not get older. They were not created with the material universe, but they did have a beginning. Kreeft reminds the reader that *aeveternity*, a word coined by philosophers of the Middle Ages, refers to angel time. Possibly this word is a convoluted way of saying that these thinkers just could not pinpoint when the heavens or angels were created.

The argument had been clearly made that when the Bible tells us that the heavens and the earth were created, this was a beginning in time, a starting in order to finish a day called day one. Furthermore, because angels were created for the benefits of God's purposes for mankind, the heavens in which they dwell and they themselves began at a specific designated time on the very first day. The fact that heaven is a place with dimensions supports the notion that the heavens and angels were created at the same time at the beginning of time.

1e. Earth

The Bible helps us understand that the earth (or we might say the universe) started out as a bounded space with water surrounding it. Just what kind of water that was is perhaps unsettled and debatable. The Hebrew word **mayim** can be translated water or transitory things (Mayim 2014). If the space was an abyss or deep space with a surrounding boundary, separating it from a spiritual heaven, then presumably the boundary had a rather spiritual nature. It could be thought of as a substance having the potential to become natural material—a boundary separating the space created by God from the boundless Creator. Because the Holy Spirit hovered over it suggests there was a heavenly sphere surrounding the material sphere. Just what separated heaven from earth at this early stage in the creation of the earth is open to interpretation. It does appear to separate spiritual from material.

Dobberpuhl (p. 48, 2011) sees the waters as a "watery universal substance" or "perfect fluid material that continues to change form." He (pp. 20-22, 2011) explains that scientists now know that pre-atomic material made up of particles like quarks and gluons exhibits perfect fluidity with low viscosity. Dobberpuhl proposes that God made both photons and atomic particles including protons, electrons, and neutrons from this substance.

To digress momentarily, we should not call this preatomic material "chaos." Chaos means confused or unorganized, but this "quark soup" has the extraordinary potential to become matter and energy in response to God's commands. It stands in a ready state. We'll return to this in section 2c.

Incidentally, there is scripture that suggests *why* God is not plainly giving us the history of creating the spiritual heavens in the first book of Genesis. He is only giving us details about the creation of earth in Genesis 1 and also in Genesis 2. Jesus spoke of the limited understanding of man's mind in regards to earthly things, but even more so in regards to heavenly things.

John 3:12 says, I have told you earthly things, and ye believe not, how shall ye believe, if I tell you of heavenly things?

As we move from heaven to earth and to the latter part of Genesis 1:2, we are moving from that which is higher to that which is lower in a hierarchy of Rulership with God as the One Supreme Ruler. There are scriptures from the Psalms that give this image of

God being above, above the heavens, above the waters, and above the sky or the earth's atmosphere.

A verse from Psalm 68 tells us that the Almighty Who we must praise, the One who rides on the heavens (or clouds), is named by the Holy Name JAH or YAH. The Christian Message Board (barrykind 2010) stated, The mystery attached to the Name of the Almighty, is related to the verb "to be" (I am, I was, I will be) which is the Hebrew verb "Hoveh"...YHVH [JAH] therefore, means... "YAH is..." So Psalm 68:4 portrays the Lord God, the Great I Am, as being above the heavens. Psalm 68:33 also paints an image of God being above the heavens and speaking with a mighty voice. This verse taken with Psalm 29:3 allows the reader to see God as above the heavens, above the waters, speaking the light into existence by the power of His word. By the power of His word, the creation is accomplished.

Psalm 8:1 says, ... who [our Lord] hast set thy glory above the heavens.

Psalm 29:3 says, The voice of the Lord is upon the waters; the God of glory thunders; the Lord is upon many waters.

Psalm 68:4 says, Sing unto God, sing praises to His name: extol Him that rideth upon the heavens by His name JAH, and rejoice before Him.

Psalm 68:33 says, To Him that rideth upon the heavens of heavens, which were of old; lo, He doth send out His voice, and that a mighty voice.

Psalm 104:3 says, Who layeth the beams of His chambers in the waters: Who maketh the clouds His chariot: Who walketh upon the wings of the wind:

As we move to the area below the surface of the waters, we move to the surface of the deep. Perhaps the waters are as seen from heaven; then below the waters is the darkness seen over the surface of the deep. We have moved into the realm of the physical universe, which the Bible tells us is unformed and unfilled. The words here are *toho* and *bohu* in Hebrew. These words have been discussed in many various authors' writings (a number cited by Fields 1976). Weston Fields named his critique of the gap theory

Unformed and Unfilled. Fields (p. 113, 1976) states that *bohu* was translated "the primaeval earth" by the *Brown, Driver, and Briggs Lexicon*, and that *tohu* was translated formlessness or emptiness. Fields stated that *tohu c*ould be thought of as an "empty outer-space." Weston Fields makes a relatively lengthy case in his chapter on *tohu* and *bohu* for this image being of an elementary unfinished substance. He did agree to some extent with the traditionalists like Martin Luther (p. 130, Fields 1976) who conceived of it as shapeless mass to which God added light later. Fields disagreed with the gap theorists who conceived of it as a chaos or disorganized mass that had become that way because it had come under God's judgment.

Consistent with this substance being some primordial or elementary material that could be used to create other things is the verse telling what God did on the third day. The waters themselves that were below the firmament brought forth living fish and birds. This implies the waters or transitory substance had the potential to miraculously become living creatures. Also consistent with this idea is II Peter 3:5 translated in the NIV telling us that the earth itself could have been formed from this water. It did not just appear as the waters drained off into the ocean, but it formed from the water. However, the KJV and the Geneva Bible are translated that the earth appeared out of the water. So we cannot be certain what this verse actually conveys. Did the water form the earth? Or did the earth emerge or appear out of the waters? It is certainly not clear.

Genesis 1:20 says, And God said, Let the waters bring forth abundantly the moving creature that hath life, and fowl that may fly above the earth in the open firmament of heaven.

II Peter 3:5 (KJV) says, For this they willingly are ignorant of, that by the word of God the heavens were of old, and **the earth standing out of the water** and in the water:

II Peter 3:5 (NIV) says, But they deliberately forget that long ago by God's word the heavens came into being and **the earth was formed out of water** and by water.

II Peter 3:5 (*Geneva Bible*) says, For this they willingly know not, that the heavens were of old, and the *earth that was of the water**, and by the water, by the word of God (with footnote: **which appeared when the waters were gathered together into one place*).

So if this was an empty space, what kind of empty space was it? In the physical universe that we know today there is only a vacuum if the space is in the process of having pressure being removed from the space, in order to maintain its emptiness. In order for this to have physically existed, there had to have been a secure absolute barrier between the space and what is outside the space. This was a space securely held in God's hand. This idea was put forth by the Jewish rabbis (pp. 20-21, Finkel, 1996). God removed Himself, viz., His Shekinah glory, from a space to make the creation. If God surrounds the creation, the image of it being held in His hand is appropriate.

Isaiah 40:12 says, Who hath measured the waters in the hollow of His hand, and meted out heaven with the span, and comprehended the dust of the earth in a measure, and weighed the mountains in scales, and the hills in a balance?

The commentator Henricus Renckens (1964) said the importance of the *bohu* and *tohu* is to indicate there was nothing there initially. This is consistent with there being darkness in this space. Renckens (b. 1908) was a Jesuit theologian at *Maastricht University* in the Netherlands. Renckens (pp. 82-84, 1964) said, **"Indeed the whole purpose of his [the author of Genesis] is to emphasize that there is nothing whatever that is outside the sphere of God's almighty power... this *tohu-wa-bohu* is in reality nothing more or less than a very concrete way of saying 'absolutely nothing whatever.'"**

In other words, Renckens' view was that God created a space with nothing in it. He was of the mindset that this version of creation in Genesis was to be strongly contrasted with the cosmology of the Mesopotamian legends that put forth the creation of gods who then proceeded to create the universe. An example is the *Enuma elish* that told about the creation of mother and father substances (or the chaos) who then created other gods, who then in the midst of battle created the universe.

The Jewish writers Rav-Noy and Weinreich (p. 70, 2010) agree that *tohu* and *bohu* signify a space with nothing in it. They translated Genesis 1:1-3 as, **"In the beginning Elokim created the heaven and the earth. And the earth was astonishingly empty with darkness upon the surface of the deep, and the Divine Presence hovered upon the surface of the waters. And Elokim said, 'Let there be light.'"**

An insightful interpretation of the words unformed and un-filled has been given by Giacinto Butindaro (2010). He expressed that the basic structure of the earth had been created by God before Genesis 1:2. Butindaro is of the opinion that the earth was covered with water at that stage. Unformed means that it did not have features that we know of today – land, sea, mountains; i.e., it was unformed. Furthermore, it was not yet filled with birds, fish, animals, and man; i.e., it was not yet filled with living creatures. We can surmise that this might be the case because in verses nine and ten, the waters were gathered together to make seas, and the dry land appeared or if it emerged presumably it was already created.

John Whitcomb (pp. 124-125, 1972) in one of his earlier works described the condition of earth in verse 2 as similar to Butindaro's appraisal of early earth. Whitcomb said, **"It is true that the earth was empty as far as living things are concerned, and it was devoid of many of the interesting features it later possessed, such as continents, mountains, rivers and seas; but it was certainly not chaotic, ruined, or judged... The earth had a core, mantle, and crust composed of perfect metal and rock, and it was covered with oceans of perfect water; and it was surrounded by a blanket of perfect atmosphere!"**

So Genesis 1:2 portrays God hovering over something that **will become** or **was** the earth (or perhaps the whole cosmos or universe). Whether the earth at this stage was either

1) some watery substance or

2) nothing (a space) bounded by a watery substance or

3) earth matter covered with water, is arguably of lesser importance than that there is no concrete scriptural evidence that a judgment had taken place either before or just after Genesis 1:1. This will be discussed in the section following on the different gap theories.

Let us reflect upon the darkness spoken of in Genesis 1:2. When there is no light, then there is darkness. Since God said let there be light, then there was light; we know that prior to that there was darkness. There was darkness on the face of the abyss. Even though darkness is often associated with evil in Bible passages, the darkness itself is not necessarily evil. It is simply the absence of light.

Matthew 6:23 says, But if thine eye be evil, thy whole body shall be full of darkness.

How does the evil become associated with darkness? If light is good, then perhaps darkness is not good. We can hide in the dark, but that does not make the darkness evil. The evil is what is being hidden in the darkness. We cannot see in the darkness with the body's eyes; eyes need light to see. Therefore, if we want to see, light is good and helpful. Not only is darkness the absence of light, God said that He created darkness as well as evil in Isaiah 45. But, God is not evil. How could He create evil?

John 3:19 says, And this is the condemnation, that light is come into the world, and men loved darkness rather than light, because their deeds were evil.

John 11:10 says, But if a man walk in the night, he stumbleth, because there is no light in him.

Isaiah 45:7 says, I form the light, and create darkness: I make peace, and create evil: I the Lord do all these things.

If there is created light, then there is the possibility of darkness. We must remember God is not evil; He is only good. However, if there is anyone less than Him created in His image; i.e., with a will and thus a choice, then there must be the possibility of obedience or disobedience. Morgenstern (pp. 38-39, 1965) wrote, **"...Judaism has never taught the absolute existence of evil alongside of good ...only through man's misuse of God's gifts...does evil come."** James explains that God is never tempted by evil, and He never tempts anyone to do evil. A person disobeys because of his will – he chooses to disobey. In the book of James we read that God gives only good and perfect gifts. God dwells in light, but He knows what is in the darkness.

James 1:13 says, Let no man say when he is tempted, I am tempted of God: for God cannot be tempted with evil, neither tempteth He any man:

1 John 1:5b says, that God is light, and in Him is no darkness at all.

Daniel 2:22 says, He revealeth the deep and secret things: He knoweth what is in the darkness, and the light dwelleth with Him.

Passages in the book of Job with God speaking to Job explain when darkness was created and the purpose of darkness. Darkness was over the deep before the earth began to take shape.

Job 38:8-15 says, Or who shut up the sea with doors, when it brake forth, as if it had issued out of the womb? When I made the cloud the garment thereof, and thick darkness a swaddlingband for it, And brake up for it my decreed place, and set bars and doors, And said, Hitherto shalt thou come, but no further: and here shall thy proud waves be stayed? Hast thou commanded the morning since thy days; and caused the dayspring to know his place; That it might take hold of the ends of the earth, that the wicked might be shaken out of it? It is turned as clay to the seal; and they stand as a garment. And from the wicked their light is withholden, and the high arm shall be broken.

This conveys there needed to be limits set on material elements, e.g., the seas, as well as other ethereal elements, like wickedness. There is a time of day and a time of night. God explains that morning has a place (and it follows that morning would have a time). The passage goes on to say that morning takes the earth by its edges. The light moves across the surface of the earth making morning, then day. The daylight reveals the deeds of mankind. It reveals the deeds of the wicked. The scripture explains that the wicked are denied their light. This suggests that even though the wicked could choose to have light (it is "theirs"), they choose evil and so are denied light.

Job 38:19 says, Where is the way where light dwelleth? and as for darkness, where is the place thereof…

The darkness could be thought of as a covering over the primordial space that was to become the completed cosmos. The darkness as seen from below caused the heavens to be clothed with darkness (Isaiah 50:3). There were waters (said to be seas here) that were confined to a space, or they were the covering over the space as seen from above – as seen from heaven's vantage point. Then as light was commanded to come into this world, it became morning or dawn (the dayspring), and light was given for life, and light was also given to reveal the wickedness that seeks to hide in the dark.

Darkness was also given for rest. The darkness was named night. Rest and sleep are good things given by God. Psalm 127:2 says that God gives His beloved sleep. Passages from Psalm 104 reveal that man works during the day and rests at night, whereas many animals hunt at night.

Psalm 104:20, 22-23 say, Thou makest darkness, and it is night: wherein all the beasts of the forest do creep forth… The sun ariseth, they gather themselves together, and lay them down in their dens. Man goeth forth unto his work and to his labour until the evening.

We might ask, Why was there a tree of good and evil in the garden of Eden? This seems to be a great mystery. Sometimes the most obvious answers do not need to be given explicitly. It is obvious to any thinker that any being with a will—an angel or a human being—would have the choice to obey or disobey God who created them. There would naturally be a choice for this created being to make. God told Adam and Eve not to eat of this tree. In eating the fruit of the tree, they chose evil; they chose disobedience. After they disobeyed we are told that they wanted to hide from God among the trees of the Garden of Eden.

1f. Sabbath

Quite a number of authors have pointed out that God set a precedent for man to work six days and rest on the seventh. Stanley Jaki (p. 45, 1996) wrote that **"God is cast in the role of a worker in order to underline the importance of the Sabbath observance."** God created the spiritual heavens and the cosmos in six days. On the seventh day, He was finished, and He rested. God called this seventh day holy.

Exodus 20 records God giving of the Ten Commandments, the reader is reminded that the seventh day is holy, and not to work on that day because God Himself rested on the seventh day after He was finished creating everything.

With the giving of the Pentateuch, the Israelites received Moses' instructions to remember that God created everything that ever was in the very first week that ever was. Exodus 31 also connects keeping the Sabbath with creation.

Exodus 31:17 says, It [keeping the Sabbath] is a sign between Me and the children of Israel forever: for in six days the Lord made heaven and earth, and on the seventh day He rested, and was refreshed.

John Calvin in his *Commentary on Genesis One* (verse 5, E-Word Today, 2013) puts it forth that God accommodated His work in six days for the work week that would be established for man. He wrote, "Let us rather conclude that God himself took the space of six days, for the purpose of accommodating His works to the capacity of men."

Jeffrey Feinberg (p. 16, 1999) stated in his book *Walking Genesis!*, **"Before time began, God created space for heaven and earth. God speaks and it happens, but the number seven most stands out! Seven times the Torah reads, 'And it was so.' Seven times it is recorded, 'and God made.' Six times God speaks with approval, 'Good!' (Gen. 1:4, 10, 12, 18, 21, 25), climaxing the seventh time with 'Very Good!' (Gen. 1:31)."**

Feinberg (p. 16, 1999) also said that Adam did not enter the Shabbat rest because he Adam failed to do the work God gave him to do. Feinberg points out that Jesus warned that today's generation is like that of Noah's day, too busy for God and for watching for the coming of the Messiah.

Dennis Lindsay (p. 107, 2011) of *Christ for the Nations Institute* stated the Scripture is "saturated" with the number seven. The seventh day is the Sabbath. There are seven Jewish feasts; there are Seven Seals in Revelation. Lindsay explained that seven is the number of completion and perfection, and he provides evidence for that fact with a passage from the Psalms.

Psalm 12:6 says, The words of the Lord are pure words: as silver is tried in a furnace of Earth, purified seven times.

The Hebrews sanctified the Sabbath day as holy. They refrained from all work on that day. Morgenstern (p. 39-40, 1965 or 1919) said the instituting of the Sabbath day by God shows the exalted position of man – that God gave man the task of helping God do good. Morgenstern said that "earnest and conscientious" labor bring about good. He quotes from the Jewish prayer-book (p. 40, 1965), "He alone, who has labored well during the week, and, according to his strength, has contributed to the greater worth of humanity will enjoy the sweetness of the Sabbath."

The Book of Jubilees (Pharisaic author 2011, 1902, or 100 B.C.)—thought to be the oldest commentary on Genesis of any, Jewish or Christian; contains extensive comments about the seventh day. This last day of the week was designated as the Sabbath and was to be kept by no other nation except Israel, a people sanctified by God forever and ever (pp. 20-21, 2011). The commentary states that the angels of presence and angels of sanctification worship God along with His people Israel on that day. *Jubilees II.30-32* (p. 20, 2011) says that the Creator God kept Sabbath in the heavens before it was made known to mankind on the earth. This is consistent with our most Holy God *not* being engaged in creating before the beginning, but dwelling in unapproachable light. He began His work when time began as indicated in Genesis 1:1 as the beginning.

Further Jewish comments about the Sabbath are found in *The Zohar*, a book of unspecified authorship that became part of the

Jewish community in the Middle Ages. There is a controversy about who wrote *The Zohar* (*5 Things You Should Know About The Zohar*), **"According to all Kabbalists, and as the beginning of the book writes, The Zohar was written by Rabbi Shimon Bar Yochai (Rashbi), who lived in the 2nd and 3rd centuries CE. There are views in scholastic circles stating that The Zohar was written in the 11th century by Kabbalist Rabbi Moshe de Leon. This view was contradicted by Rabbi Moshe de Leon himself, who said that the book was written by Rashbi."**

According to *The Zohar*, the Sabbath as the last day of the week speaks of a future day at the end. In *The Zohar* (p. 152, 1933), we read, **"Rabbi Simeon said further: 'It is on this account [a tabernacle of peace comes down from heaven and is spread over the world as the Sabbath is sanctified by prayers,] that, we have learnt Sabbath is a mirror of the future world.'"**

Let us further consider what the Sabbath means to the Christian. As expressed by Clara Sauls in her book *The Christian Sabbath* (p. 97, 1976), **"Christians do have a Sabbath; and the Christian Sabbath is the Lord Jesus Christ Himself."** In Sauls' first chapter, she lists scriptures showing that Jesus established a standard for meeting with His church on the first day of the week. Jesus appeared after His resurrection to Mary Magdalene on the first day of the week (John 20:1).

On the evening of that same day, Jesus appeared in the middle of a gathering of His disciples (John 20:19).

A week later on the first day of the week, Jesus appeared to His disciples again when Thomas was present (John 20:29).

In Acts 20:7, the Bible records that the disciples met together on the first day of the week, and Paul preached to them.

Furthermore, in the last book of the New Testament, John records of receiving his revelation from God on the Lord's Day.

Clara Sauls (p. 19, 1976) wrote, **"The Lord's day is not specifically identified in this verse. I have an opinion as to what it is, but we are not dealing in opinions in this study."** Sauls says that the Bible records Jesus appeared to His disciples 14 times after His resurrection, and that the first six times were documented to be on the first day of the week.

Marvin Wilson (1989), theology professor at *Gordon College*, gives us information about when the church set rules for meeting on Sunday, although Wilson does express it is not known when the first church began to meet on Sunday, however passages in Acts 20:7 (of Paul preaching on the first day) and in I Corinthians 16:2 (of an offering to be taken on the first day), suggest that it was very early on. Wilson (p. 79, 1989) writes, **"He [Ignatius] wrote to the Magnesians [A.D. 115], telling them to 'no longer live for the Sabbath but for the Lord's Day, on which day our life arose.' *The Didache*, a manual of church instruction written about A.D. 120, also directs Christians to come together on the Lord's Day to worship."**

The author Richard Booker (p. 62, 2009) expressed that the timing of Passover, Feast of Unleavened Bread, Feast of Firstfruits, and Pentecost indicate prophetically when according to the Jewish Calendar the Messiah would become the Passover Lamb, be crucified, and then resurrected. Sauls also expresses this in her first chapter: that Firstfruits was to be held on the first day of the week, corresponding to the day of Jesus' resurrection, and that 50 days later on the first day of the week, the feast of Pentecost was to be held. These Jewish holidays are prophetic as to when the Messiah would appear to His disciples after His death, and when the Holy Spirit would be poured out upon the believers. These events were to occur on the first day of the week. The first fruits of the barley harvest (Firstfruits) and the first fruits of the wheat harvest (Pentecost) 50 days later are both celebrated on the 1st day of the week.

To backtrack for a minute, we must appreciate Professor Wilson's (p. 80, 1989) appraisal of the thought that the Jewish community over the centuries rejected Christianity because Christians rejected the Sabbath and therefore, rejected the Law and the "old covenant," replacing it with the "new covenant." Wilson went on to say that he is not advocating that the Church adopt a strict Sabbatarianism to counteract this rejection.

Patrick Madrid (p. 183-184, 2002), founder of the Catholic *Envoy Magazine*, comments that *The Didache (The Lord's Teaching through the Twelve Apostles to the Nations)* written around 100 A.D. confirms that Mass was celebrated on Sunday. Madrid states that this tradition had been established by the early Apostles, and the *Lord's Day* in Revelation was Sunday. He further comments the Catholic Church adopted Sunday as the day of worship for two reasons:

1) to commemorate the Lord's resurrection of the first day of the week, and

2) to distinguish the new Faith from the Old Covenant observance of the day of rest on the Sabbath.

The letter from Paul to the Colossians expresses it best:
Let us respect each other's beliefs in regards to holding to the Sabbath.

Colossians 2:16-17 says, Let no man therefore judge you in meat, or in drink, or in respect of an holyday, or of the new moon, or of the sabbath days: Which are a shadow of things to come; but the body is of Christ.

As for Jesus being the Sabbath, there is convincing evidence that this is the case. Just as the tabernacle and constructed temples were a type or shadow of the real temple in Heaven, so the Law (Hebrews 10:1) and the Sabbath were shadows of what was to be fulfilled.

Hebrews 8:5 says, … Moses was admonished of God when he was about to make the tabernacle: for, See, saith He, that thou make all things according to the pattern shewed to thee in the mount.

The Hebrew word Sabbath used in Genesis chapter one means **rest**. Jewish commentaries state that the designation of the seventh day as a day of rest was not explicitly expressed in Genesis, but in Exodus 20, as well as in Deuteronomy 5. In these two verses respectively, the Israelites were asked to remember to keep the Sabbath and that 1) God was the Creator, and 2) He delivered them from bondage in Egypt.

In Numbers 14 we read of the **rest** that God desired to give the Israelites on the day of provocation at Kadesh (Ch. III, Sauls, 1976) when Joshua and Caleb gave a good report. But they did not enter into that rest because of their unbelief. The letter to the Hebrews revisits that fact, warning that if one hears the message of the Gospel today, the hearer should enter into that rest without hesitation.

Hebrews 9:4-11 says, There remaineth therefore a rest to the people of God. For he that is entered into his rest, he also hath ceased from his own works, as God did from His. Let us labour therefore to enter into that rest, lest any man fall after the same example of unbelief.

Jesus told his disciples that they could be yoked with Him to rest from their labors. He also taught that the Sabbath was made for man, not man for the Sabbath (Mark 2:27). Again the Sabbath was prophetic of the **rest** that would come with Jesus fulfilling the Law and providing the perfect atonement for sin. It could also be said that it foretells the future of a heaven where there is no longer any sorrow or death or wickedness, a place of peace and rest from our labors.

Matthew 11:28 says, Come unto Me, all ye that labour and are heavy laden, and I will give you rest.

Chapter 2

Creation *Ex Nihilo*

Influential modern Christian leaders have espoused creation *ex nihilo,* and this can be verified. Two significant Christian teachers with this view, though not necessarily espousing young earth creationism, have wielded considerable influence in the 20th century. They are Peter Kreeft, Professor at Boston College, which is Catholic; and Francis Schaeffer, Protestant philosopher. Kreeft has influenced the Catholic world; Schaeffer those Christian seekers of the 20th century interested in philosophy.

Kreeft and Tacelli (p. 106, 1994) contrast the Christian idea of creation *ex nihilo* due to an infinite God with the Greek philosophers' notion of *ex nihilo nihil fit* ("out of nothing nothing comes"). The philosophical view, Kreeft says, is only because of the finite laws of nature, but God creates supernaturally. Kreeft acknowledged that the theory of evolution is "in scientific trouble," saying that scientists and philosophers do not agree about evolution. We can only hope that philosophers and theologians can have an influence on how science is used to solve various problems, or explain various questions that we have.

Francis Schaeffer describes creation *ex nihilo* as the means by which God created the universe in his writings. He (p. 25, 1968) states, **"This personal-infinite God of the Bible is the Creator of all else. God created all things, and He created them out of nothing."**

This Christian philosopher points to an impassable line or barrier between God and man because of the fall. Schaeffer reacted to the nihilistic 20th century view of man. He said that man needs to relate upward to God because of grace, but man modeled as a machine or animal is below the chasm (barrier) between the infinite and the finite. Schaeffer (p. 29, 1968) claims the line between the infinite and finite was answered by the Reformation by showing "Christ is equally Lord in both areas: grace and nature." In other words, God bridges the gap between heaven and earth and allows man access to the infinite through Christ.

Schaeffer (p. 24, 1972) in *Genesis in Space and Time* stresses that the Christian view of creation has always been *ex nihilo*. He writes, **"The historic Christian position concerned Genesis 1:1 is the only one which can be substantiated, the only one which is fair and adequate to the whole thrust of Scripture. 'In the beginning' is a technical term stating the fact that at this particular point of sequence there is a creation *ex nihilo* – a creating out of nothing. All that is, except for God himself who already has been, now comes into existence."**

Gerhard May (1978, 2004 translated from German by AS Worrall), professor of theology at *Johannes Gutenberg University*, published a treatise on the doctrine of creation *ex nihilo* developed by church fathers. Professor May presents an outline of the overlapping of ideas coming from apostolic writers, Greek thinkers like Plato and Aristotle, and Gnosticism arising from worldwide age-old religious thought. Many different religious sects arose in the first few centuries after Christ, and with them many numerous and varied doctrines. The idea of creation of everything from nothing by an Almighty Creator was defended by early church fathers who wrote against what they declared to be diverse heresies.

Karl Barth and Emil Brunner, Swiss contemporaries of each other in early 20th century represent neo-Orthodoxy (discussed in the next few paragraphs). They defended God as creator as portrayed in scripture; not in nature. Barth emphasized creation is only understood as part of God's covenant with man; understood by faith. Brunner emphasized creation is only understood by revelation. The similarities between these two Swiss theologians are much greater than any differences.

Barth and Brunner did not challenge the escalating evolutionary theory of their time. Nevertheless, both of them stressed a gulf between science and theology (cf. pp. 93-94, Poe and Davis 2012). Poe and Davis state that neo-Orthodoxy was a "retreat from theological engagement with science." E. J. Young (p. 32, 1976) explained that Barth's modern religion puts theology into a "noumenal" realm, whereas science remains in the realm of phenomenon. The noumenal here means a reality behind the ability to observe and measure. However, even E.J. Young seems to have misinterpreted Barth's idea of creation *ex nihilo*; Barth emphasized creation *ex nihilo* was more than what he called a "theologoumenon" or a theological principle; it is a most important article of faith based on biblical insight (p. 157, Barth 1960). Barth emphasized that creation can only be understood in the light of the love of God expressed through Jesus Christ. Man was created to be in relationship with God as expressed in the Bible (cf. pp. 27-30, Gabriel 2014).

By the way, theologians Harry Lee Poe and Jimmy Davis (2012) hold to an intelligent design scenario. Their primary aim appears to be to reveal that process theology as represented by someone like Teilhard de Chardin (1881-1955) is not compatible with the Biblical narrative. In process theology (p. 90, Bonting 2005), the universe undergoes self-determination; life itself makes choices, especially the human who has a will and choices to be made.

Attempts to bring theology and science together have been made by modern theologians; e.g., Bonting (p. 15, p. 94, 2005), a retired Dutch biochemist and Anglican priest, proposed a chaos theology. Bonting stated that at the beginning there needed to be something; a chaos must be at least an "existing nothing" to be scientifically accurate. He accepts a precreation "immaterial-rich chaos," which is the substance existing at the time of the big bang, t=0. He asserts this is the Biblical view. A longer discussion of precreation chaos is given below in section 3c.

Sjoerd Bonting (pp. 70-72, 2005) claimed both Barth and Brunner thought it was an existing nothing (*nihil ontologicum*), not an absolute nothing (*nihil negativum*). As it turns out, Bonting was incorrect in saying that Barth and Brunner held to an existing nothing; they did not. The erudite writings of these two greats of theology have been misinterpreted by Bonting, as they have been by others. For this study, we are primarily interested in these two men's interpretations of creation expressed in Biblical texts, not their rejection of philosophical models of origins.

Brunner (p. 10, 1952) said, **"The truth that God is the One who determines all things and is determined by none, is the precise meaning of the idea of Creation as *creation ex nihilo*. Creation 'out of nothing' does not mean, however—as Gnosticism of all ages continually interprets it—that there was once a 'Nothing' out of which God created the world, a negative primal beginning, a Platonic ME ON, a formlessness, a chaos, a primal Darkness... There never was a 'nothing' alongside of God, as it were, but God alone. The Gnostic doctrine of 'Nothing' is the final attempt to adapt the certainly incomprehensible mystery of Creation to that which we know from experience as a semi-creation, the formation of something; it understands the Creation as the moulding of a formless original substance."**

Brunner stressed that philosophy and theology cannot arrive at creation *ex nihilo*; it is a concept that must be revealed to man by God. Creation must have been accomplished supernaturally; therefore, the procedures of creation cannot be explained using natural laws. Barth and Brunner willingly relinquished their chance to speak theologically about scientific matters.

Barth also stressed that creation *ex nihilo* was implicit in the story of creation in Genesis, and it stands opposed to

1) creation being an emanation of the divine being (monism) or

2) to an independent entity eternally co-existing with God (dualism). Barth stated, **"...the doctrine of *creation ex nihilo* has its [sic] root in Hebrew and not in Greek thought"** (p. 155, 1960).

Karl Barth and Emil Brunner, like the Reformers who spoke in the century before them, came to the conclusion that man's mind is also fallen, as was pointed out by Francis Schaeffer. Science has its limits: in attempting to answer questions about absolutes and supernatural events like creation in six days, it is doomed to come up with inadequate answers.

Bonting (p. 104, 2005) believes the precreation chaos is being reduced as creation continues because the Creator can add energy and information into the universe over time, thereby decreasing entropy (= chaos). The problem with Bonting's idea is that creation would not be finished on the seventh day; it continues even today and on into the future. Other problems are whether entropy is actually decreasing and evolution taking place. This has not been verified. Process theology also has creation continuing into the future; Chardin has an Omega point at which man will have reached his summit and be like Christ. Perhaps both process theology and chaos theology are entirely different gospels, so to speak; and they are invalid interpretations of the Bible.

Stanley Jaki, Benedictine priest born in Hungary, writes about the futile attempts by early church fathers and those that followed up to today to make science and the Bible fit together (pp. 46-48, 1996). Jaki wrote, **"Appreciation of the fact that the thrust of God's creative work is the all [totum per partes], might, if properly appreciated, have served as a power antidote against the ever present lure of setting up a concordance between Genesis 1 and the science of the day. ...The Church Fathers ...[tried] trying to make it appear that the cosmos and cosmogenesis of Genesis 1 closely parallel the data of Greek science and astronomy. The Scholastics, with Thomas Aquinas... claimed a concordance to exist between Genesis 1 and Aristotle's physics. This mistaken approach was vigorously cultivated by the exegetes of the Counter-Reformation and quickly assimilated by Protestants, who... could not live with Luther's and Calvin's precepts... concerning Genesis 1."**

A number of passages from the New Testament confirm that God created everything, which includes spiritual heavens, earth, outer space, as well as any substance from whence material things were created. One such passage is given below from Hebrews. A house that is built is made from boards and so forth, but God built the house and made the boards too. God did this supernaturally. This will be further considered in the section below on the traditional view in section 2c.

Hebrews 3:4 says, For every house is builded by some man; but He that built all things is God.

2a. Creation of Heavenly Heavens and Cosmos on Day One

Everything created including angels and the heavenly heavens was created in six days. This view is supported by this exposition.

In order for God to create man and angels with the potential for both knowledge and immortality, God needed to establish a kingdom with Himself as Ruler. The Word was and is Ruler – the only begotten Son is the Word. If God made absolute rules, then He Himself would submit to the rules that were established. He swore by Himself and confirmed it with an oath (Hebrews 6:18).

Psalm 103:19 says, The Lord hath prepared His throne in the heavens; and His kingdom ruleth over all.

John 1:1 says, … and the Word was God.

The potential for knowledge was represented by the tree of knowledge of good and evil. The potential for immortality was represented as the tree of life. God commanded Adam not to eat of the tree of knowledge. Furthermore, man was told to rule over the created animals and earth. Whether it was an earthly snake influenced by the devil, or the devil appearing as a snake as some have suggested, Adam and Eve had been commanded to rule over it. The snake lied saying that they would not die if they ate of the tree, and that God did not want them to have knowledge because then they would be like Him. The snake implied that God wanted to have absolute control over them and was withholding knowledge from them. The snake accused God, and the devil carried out his deceitful plot to cause man's downfall. Man was to rule over the snake.

God supernaturally made all things in six days, including His heavenly throne and Lucifer too. Many Bible scholars have proposed that the devil did not fall until after the creation was completed. This is consistent with the thought that as Satan observed the creation of man and understood man's position as ruler over the earth. Satan's appointed position was to obey and worship God and help man learn to obey and worship God, but he became prideful and jealous. He did not like the idea of submitting to God's authority. It was then that he fell, conjuring up a plan to cause man's defeat. His fall could be said to be at the beginning of history.

Let us look at creation *ex nihilo* in more detail by reading in Nehemiah. Nehemiah 9:5-6 records the Levites encouraging the Israelites to worship the God who alone made the heaven, the heaven of heaven with all their hosts (angels who also worship Him), the earth and the sea. In this passage God is also identified as the One who chose Abraham. This inclusive tribute to God who all by Himself created it all indicates that all creation was done as one unit. God created the heavens and the earth.

Dr. Feinberg (p. 17, 1998), a leader of a Messianic congregation in Illinois, cites *The Pentateuch and Rashi Commentary* edited by Ben Avraham and others. **"Rashi says that everything was created (in potential) on the first day, but the actual generating takes place on the days that follow."** Feinberg also expressed that God walled off heaven on the second day (with the waters above) and did not proclaim "Good!" for that day's work. Feinberg speculated that God reserved heaven for His place of rest, and it was walled off from man's domain because God foreknew that man would live on earth in a fallen state. Feinberg (p. 16, p. 25, 1998) says that man did not enter into the Sabbath rest, nor did the Israelites enter God's rest because of their unbelief.

John Gill, Baptist theologian born in 1697 in England, believed the angels were created on day one along with their abode (the heavens) (Introduction, B3, C2, Gill 1767). Gill believed the angels that fell with the devil (now demons) did not fall until after the six days of creation because on the sixth day God said all He had created was very good (Genesis 1:31) (s.2b, B3, C5, 1767).

Gill distinguished the first day's **immediate** creation of heaven (with angels), from earth and light created on the following five days that he called **mediate** creation of all things from "pre-existent matter, which of itself was not disposed to produce them [these things]" (s.1, B3, C1, 1767). Gill supported his interpretation of creation *ex nihilo*, i.e., from nothing with Revelation 4:11. God's goodness was manifested as His will to create.

Revelation 4:11 says, ... for thou hast created all things, and for thy pleasure they are and were created.

2b. Were Angels Created before Genesis 1:1 or Outside Time?

Those that espouse creation of the angels before the beginning feel that the Bible does not tell us when the angels were created. Then they proceed to support their tenuous conclusions with various ideas.

Well-known Christian teachers like Billy Graham embrace creation of the universe from nothing, but believe angels were created before the beginning. Herbert Lockyer Jr. wrote *All the Angels in the Bible* in 1995 to help reawaken interest particularly in Christians, of angels as portrayed in the Bible. He believed angels were created much earlier than the cosmos. Lockyer (pp. 13-14, 1995) said, **"... the time, order, place, and manner of the creation of the noblest and most exalted creatures of God are not revealed... Angelic beings then, we confidently conclude, were created long before the foundation of the earth. But just when...is not a subject of divine revelation."**

Others have suggested that angels were created outside of our time domain. Peter Kreeft (pp. 92-93, 1995) wrote of this possibility; and tells the reader that this angel time has been called *aeveternity* by Medieval philosophers—they proposed that it had a beginning but no ending. Kreeft said angels were assuredly not created at the same time as the material universe (he holds to a Big Bang at the beginning). I believe John Gill (s.2a1, B3, C1, 1767) would counter this idea with his notion of heaven being a place where there are resurrected human bodies, such as the bodies of the resurrected Jesus, and Elijah and Enoch, and that it was built by God (Hebrews 11:10) and therefore was made in time.

2c. Traditional View (Originally Perfect Yet Incomplete Theory)

The traditional view of the Christian church has been creation *ex nihilo*, as expressed above. It also has been called the initial chaos theory by some, because the incomplete substance from which God created has been termed "chaos." There sometimes has been proposed a soft-like time gap between Genesis 1:1 and 1:3. In other words, God created heaven and earth—the earth then being some substance described in Genesis 1:2 that existed, and was used to create everything else. Some believe this may not have begun immediately after the substance being earth was created; that is, the subsequent creating may not have begun on the very next day.

God supernaturally created heaven at the very start, and then earth was supernaturally created by God in six days. The six days of creation of earth was appropriate because those beings, viz., humans, appointed to rule earth would rule in the format of a six-day work week with one day of rest. Likewise the heavens were created in an instant with angels to rule by God's commands, beyond the realm of earthly time or space. Oh, the richness of the wisdom of God, that so much could be contained in the first verse of the Bible.

Two English theologians at the turn of the 18th century supported this view. Matthew Henry (1662-1714) and John Gill (1697-1771) explicitly expressed the traditional view that God created substance on the first day, then light, and completed the creation on the remaining five days of a six-day creation. Henry (Genesis 1:1, II. 1., 1714) said the first matter was what he called "chaos," called "earth" in the Bible because as a heavy unwieldy massive substance it resembled what would later be called earth on the third day. It was called deep, Henry said, because it was so vast. The darkness that was present before the light was not created; it was purely the absence of light—the light that had not been created yet. John Gill believed the spiritual heavens, angels, and some sort of pre-existent matter (in the sense of not being matter yet) used to create the material universe were all created on the first day (see section 2c above). Even though Henry called this first matter "chaos," the argument has been made this is an inappropriate word for it because this first substance had extraordinary potential to become matter and energy.

Bruce Waltke (1975) and Mark Rooker (1992a, 1992b) have dissected the first few verses of Genesis over and over again. They are not the only ones that have scrutinized these verses, in English, in Greek, and in Hebrew, and in many different translations. Does the use of the phrase "heaven and earth" in the first verse refer to the same thing as it does in other passages of Scripture? Is it a merism? Is it a totality? It's been asked: how can "heaven and earth" refer to a completed spiritual heaven and an incomplete earth as it begins a chronological sequence? It is likely that that is exactly what it refers to.

This exposition proposes that "heaven and earth" refers to a totality created by God over six days, with day one allowing a completion of the creation of heaven and a start of the creation of earth. This view is supported by Genesis 1:1 and Genesis 2:4 starting and ending, respectively, the records of the steps God took to create it all. When the supernatural creating had been accomplished, God stopped creating, declared it very good, and rested. In other passages found in the Old and New Testaments, the merism "heaven and earth" refers to the totality of all that God created! This merism conveys everything, all things, those being both spiritual and material. Furthermore, the scripture in Job declaring that the angels rejoiced when as the foundations of the earth were laid could be interpreted as occurring at the beginning of time in Genesis 1:1. The heavens with all the angels were created, and the foundations of the earth were laid as the angels rejoiced. Establishing the foundations allowed the created substance to occupy a space, but it had not yet been transformed or made into energy (light) and atomic matter. It was unformed and not yet shaped or expanded (unfilled), and it was dark.

Job 38:4-7 says, Where wast thou when I laid the foundations of the earth? Declare, if thou hast understanding. Who hath laid the measures thereof, if thou knowest? or Who hath stretched the line upon it? Whereupon are the foundations thereof fastened? or Who laid the corner stone thereof; When the morning stars sang together, and all the sons of God shouted for joy?

Bruce Waltke (p. 219, 1975) analyzes various critiques of the initial chaos theory, attempting to show their fallacies. But his analyses can also be criticized. He said that Calvin's interpretation was not valid because Calvin maintained that "heaven and earth" referred to a confused mass that God called water, but everywhere else in scripture "heaven and earth" referred to an ordered universe. Perhaps Calvin slipped up when he thought heaven and earth were both being designated as empty and void, and that it was just the earthly or material realm being so designated. However, the heavens of verse one referred to spiritual heavens. Waltke cites Boyer (1933) and Konig (1925) who both suggested that heavens were the "completed upper heavens, including the angelic realm," and that the earth is not completed in verse two. Then Waltke dismisses this idea as "unconvincing." Agreeing with Boyer and Konig, we could ask: how many times are we going to go over this?

Consistent with this idea of spiritual heavens and earthly earth, Psalm 33 can be interpreted as God creating heaven and earth as recorded in Genesis 1:1. By God's word alone, the heavens were made along with all the angels by His breath; He made the "waters" – substance stored in a deep space to be used to make all materials including even mankind.

Psalm 33:6-9 says, By the word of the Lord were the heavens made; and all the host of them by the breath of His mouth. He gathereth the waters of the sea together as an heap: He layeth up the depth in storehouses. Let all the earth fear the Lord: let all the inhabitants of the world stand in awe of Him. For He spake, and it was done; He commanded, and it stood fast.

It is interesting that Waltke (p. 224, 1975) concludes that since according to his analyses both Christian and Jewish tradition held that the first verse is independent, and that therefore God did not create chaos, then chaos must have preexisted. Waltke's appraisal of verse one as independent is correct, but that does not make it necessary that chaos must have preexisted. Verse two gives additional information about the earth, allowing verse one to be an introductory statement with a chronological order following it, leading up to Genesis 2:4 as a final summary.

Incidentally, Martin Luther (cited by Waltke 1975) seems to have interpreted the shapeless mass as being the material heaven and earth, like Calvin also did. Luther said, **"This was not unlike a shapeless crude seed from which things can be generated and produced."**

It is Waltke (p. 217, 1975) and Rooker (p. 318, 1992a), who provide references to other scholars that agree with the initial chaos theory (originally perfect yet incomplete theory) – including Calvin, Luther, the authors of the grammatical analysis of *Gesenius' Hebrew Grammar*, Hartom and Cassuto (who together published a Biblical commentary written in Hebrew), along with Edward J. Young. Waltke's footnote about Young expresses some hesitation to admit that Young believed God created the substance described in verse two.

There seems to be no doubt that Professor E. J. Young believed in a six-day creation from nothing. In reading Young's last comments about creation, it is apparent that he believed in an absolute beginning and absolute creation from nothing (pp. 22-25, Young 1976). In 1968, the last year of his life, Professor Young, who had taught for 30 years at *Westminster Theological Seminary* in Philadelphia, gave a series of visiting lectures to *Toronto Baptist Seminary* students. In these lectures, Young proclaimed that he agreed with Julius Wellhausen, a German theologian who published at the turn of the 20th century, on the matter of absolute creation. Wellhausen felt that anything other than a six-day creation was "desperate." Young said he agreed with that conclusion. The chaos, explained Young, was simply the "original unformed state of the earth." Pertaining to this matter, Young said that he agreed with Gerhard von Rad (p. 29, Young 1976), who viewed the initial state as unfinished. In *Genesis: A Commentary* (p. 50, 1973) the translation of von Rad is, **"The assumption, however, of a cosmic Luciferlike plunge of the creation from its initial splendor is linguistically and objectively quite impossible."** In other words, von Rad did not accept the ruin-restitution theory.

The *Geneva Bible* of 1599 conveys the viewpoint that God created heaven and earth from nothing; earth was an "unformed lump" covered with water that was used to create the material cosmos. The waters above were the clouds. This interpretation alludes to this taking place within the first two days. Here are the verses 1-8 of Genesis 1 with the footnotes in italic.

1:1 In the [a] beginning God created the heaven and the earth.

> (a) *First of all, and before any creature was, God made heaven and earth out of nothing.*

1:2 And the earth was [b] without form, and void; and [c] darkness [was] upon the face of the deep. And the Spirit of God [d] moved upon the face of the waters.

> (b) *As an unformed lump and without any creature in it: for the waters covered everything.*

> (c) *Darkness covered the deep waters, for the waters covered everything.*

> (d) *He maintained this disordered mass by his secret power.*

1:3 And God said, Let there be light: and there was [e] light.

> (e) *The light was made before either Sun or Moon was created: therefore we must not attribute that to the creatures that are God's instruments, which only belong to God.*

1:7 And God made the firmament, and divided the waters which [were] [f] under the firmament from the waters which [were] above the firmament: and it was so.

> (f)   As the sea and rivers, from those waters that are in
> the clouds, which are upheld by God's power, least
> they should overwhelm the world.

1:8   And God called the firmament [g] Heaven. And the evening
and the morning were the second day.

> (g)   That is, the region of the air, and all that is above us.

Another Christian teacher who has influenced Christian students preparing to go on the mission field is Dennis Lindsay, President of *Christ for the Nations Institute* (CFTN). Although his father Gordon Lindsay taught the "gap theory," Dennis evaluated the theories carefully, and has been a young earth creationist since the early '70s (Lyons 2006). He has written 17 volumes of a pocketbook series called *Creation Science Series*, published from 1990-2011, and CFTN now houses a "Museum of Earth History."

For the sake of being complete, mention should be made of a modern creation *ex nihilo* theory. However, the theory held by Jurgen Moltmann does not accept a six-day creation. Bonting (pp. 72-73, 2005) explains that Moltmann invokes from Jewish mysticism:

1) a withdrawing of God into Himself and

2) a contraction of His Shekinah glory. God creates a space from which He empties Himself.

Bonting and several other theologians (Bonting names David Fergusson and Alan Torrance) find this theory to be what they call "unconvincing." It appears that Moltmann's picture of God's initial creation of a space is similar to that discussed by this exposition in section 1c above.

Chapter 3

Chaos Before Creation of Universe

3a. Greek Philosophers

The major Greek philosophers to be considered in regards to pre-existing matter are Plato and Aristotle. The cosmogony of Plato was quite elaborate, and it changed from his earlier to later writings. His story *Timaeus* is thought to best represent his final views. The cause of creation was "God" as the perfect soul (with perfect mind or reason), as demiurge – this eternal being is unmoved and yet self-moved. Eslick (1982) wrote, **"[this] Demiurge eternally and without change contemplates the Archetypal Model, the Eternal Forms."** The eternal soul created the cosmos (the world soul) with expressions of mathematical perfection and order, and created it out of disordered matter. He did this by creating lesser gods than himself, and they subsequently created living creatures and mankind. Men have mortal bodies, but immortal souls. If they live righteously, they can return to the particular stars from where their souls came; but if they live in an unrighteous manner, they will be reborn in "lesser bodies" (summarized from Stenudd 2010). In contrast, Aristotle understood that the cosmos was the Prime Mover itself (p. 78, Jaki 1996). He maintained that the cosmos was created as the disorder reacted to the divine order of the perfect soul.

It has been said that Church fathers adopted many aspects of the thinking of the Greek philosophers. St. Augustine (4th century) wrote extensively about the doctrines of the Church, and many aspects of his thinking appeared to be derived from Plato. An example is his concept of God being eternal, immutable, and perfect (p. 112, Torcia 1999). However, both the Bible and the Greek philosophers just inadvertently describe these similar characteristics of their ultimate god, but these are not the same gods. Perhaps Plato and Aristotle borrowed to some degree these descriptions of their demiurge from even older Judaic sources. Furthermore, Augustine did not accept pre-existing matter (p. 53, Bixler 1999, p. 109, Torcia 1999); he believed in creation *ex nihilo*.

The Roman Catholic Church designates St. Augustine and St. Thomas Aquinas (12th century) as leading founders of their creed. Aquinas emphasized both Plato's universals like Augustine, but gave equal credence to particulars like Aristotle (p. 76, Poe and Davis 2012). Aristotle had an idea that pre-existing substance was attracted and conformed to the perfection of the Divine Force. However, Aquinas did not accept eternity of matter even though the Scholastics of the Middle Ages in general reawakened their philosophical roots in Aristotle.

Francis Schaeffer (p. 9-10, 1968) points out that Aquinas ushered in the modern era with the distinction of dealing with particulars in a scientific manner. Schaeffer explains that Aquinas represented the Renaissance ideas (rebirth of Hellenic thinking and Neo-Platonism), and in an important sense foretold the possibility of the Reformation (Ch .2, Schaeffer 1968). Schaeffer explains the Reformation finally dealt with the separation of universals from particulars by emphasizing the complete fall of man—his body as well as his mind, and the saving grace of God's revealed truth in Jesus Christ who atones for man's sins and raises him up to a new status like that intended for him before the fall. Schaeffer maintained the thinking of Luther and Calvin with their emphases on faith and grace allowed modern man to decisively see God as both personal and infinite and Creator of all else that exists.

Plato and Aristotle are the founders of Western philosophy. Theologians that have continued in philosophical reasoning have reached an impasse in attempting to prove creation from nothing. This was brilliantly elucidated by Emil Brunner, the Swiss theologian of the first half of the 20th century, who incidentally, accepted evolutionary thought to some extent in its early formulation. Brunner is known as a neo-Orthodox with implications that his theology could not speak about physical and natural laws; furthermore he more than satisfactorily dismisses philosophy itself as a means to understand creation from nothing which he accepted. Brunner effectively convinces the readers that philosophy cannot arrive at creation from nothing using reason. The concept of creation *ex nihilo* must come by revelation.

Brunner (pp. 11-12, 1949) writes, **"For a philosophy which is controlled by the belief that everything can be deduced by human reflection and thus assumes the absolute continuity of human thought, must be indignant about the 'fundamental error' of the idea of Creation... It is the same Word which created the world which also reveals to us the truth that the world has been created ... no philosophy – save that which begins with revelation and to which usually the very name of philosophy is denied – contains the idea of Creation, in the sense of *creation ex nihilo*. Plato's Demiurge shapes the world, but does not create it; and Aristotle teaches explicitly the eternal co-existence of God and the world (cf. Etienne Gilson, L'*esprit de la philosophie medieval).*"**

3b. Gnosticism and Nicolaitans

Gnosticism must be distinguished from Greek philosophy, although aspects of Greek thought were adopted by a number of Gnostic sects. Gnosticism describes a great number of different schools developed primarily around the time of the early church and well into the first and second centuries. There is little doubt that some of the basic tenets of Gnostic systems developed from religious sources that existed well before the time of Christ. Some originated from the Oriental thinking of India, Babylonian civilization, and Zoroastrianism prevalent in Persia. Gnosticism is syncretistic, but different sects emphasized many different ways of explaining their "so-called" truths, or *gnosis*—secret knowledge leading to salvation, freedom, or enlightenment.

The majority of Gnostic sects developing in the first and second centuries were primarily based on Christian teaching, but significantly altered and perverted. Arendzen (1909) wrote a lengthy piece for *The Catholic Encyclopedia* on Gnosticism. This author divided the schools of Gnosticism into four groups:

1) The oldest school was Syrian and included the teaching of Simon Magus. They as a group believed that Jehovah was the last of seven angels who made the world out of pre-existent matter. They "botched up" or messed up their creation of matter and man, but the transcendent God sent a spark of divinity into the hearts of men.

2) The second school was Hellenistic/Alexandrian, and the major thinkers were Basilides of Alexandria and Valentinus who opened a school in Rome about 160 A.D. (It should be noted that Irenaeus put Valentinus in the Syrian group; see more about Irenaeus below.)

3) The third school of thinking was dualistic. Marcion said the dual eternal principles were the God of the Old and the New Testaments. He was a forerunner of Hermogenes who developed his sect in Carthage in the second century, as well as of Mani and the Manicheans of the 3rd century. Dualists viewed the opponent of the good God as eternal matter—the source of evil.

4) The fourth school, wrote Arendzen, was antinomian and primarily concerned with opposing the moral law. The Nicolaites (or Nicolaitans or Nicolaitanes) were antinomian and had existed since the time of the early Church. There is considerable evidence from writings by Irenaeus and Origen that this sect originated with the followers of Nicolas, one of the seven deacons written about in Acts 6:5.

Nicolaitans had three heretical practices according to *Smith's Bible Dictionary* (p. 218, 1979). **"They held it lawful to eat food sacrificed to idols; to join in idolatrous worship; and that God did not create the universe."** The fact that they did not believe in God as creator would substantiate that they were a Gnostic sect.

In Book I of *Against Heresies*, Irenaeus speaks against this heresy. Irenaeus said that this sect did not hold to any moral codes. Nicolaitans exhibited unrestrained indulgence. Irenaeus wrote that the Apocalypse of John, referring to Revelation, indicated that Nicolaitans practiced adultery and ate food sacrificed to idols. Irenaeus also referred to Christ speaking of this group in Revelation, and that Jesus the Christ hated their deeds.

In Book 3 of *Against Heresies*, Irenaeus specifically refutes this group's heresy by referring to passages from St. John's Gospel. John sought to remove this error, wrote Irenaeus, by proclaiming God created all things by His Word who is His Son. Nicolaitans "are an offset of that knowledge falsely so-called," said Irenaeus. Basically this sect describes a Christ who was not resurrected, but a spiritual self who flew back to the Pleroma (transcendental spiritual realm according to Gnosticism) from the cross on which the man Jesus of Nazareth was crucified. As we can easily see, this is an entirely different gospel than the one preached by Paul.

Galatians 1:8 says, But though we, or an angel from heaven, preach any other gospel unto you than that which we have preached unto you, let him be accursed.

Arendzen also documented that Origen refuted this school of thinking and the Nicolaitans in particular, as those who were solemnly obliged to break the moral codes of the Jews. Origen wrote that their basic principle was "*parachresthai te sarki*," which translates "to actively pursue the lust of the flesh" (section on Gnosticism, Alfred 2014). This group of Antinomian Gnostics was notorious for their bad moral conduct, and according to Justin, Irenaeus, and the historian Eusebius, "the reputation of these men brought infamy upon the whole race of Christians" (under (d) The Antinomian School, Arendzen 1909).

Footnote #4 from the online commentary on Revelation (citing from the book *Revelation 1-7*, Garland 2014) has this to say, **"'The explanation that takes the Nicolaitans to be composed of followers of Nicolaus of Antioch has strong support in the early church. Added to Irenaeus are the testimonies of Tertullian, Hippolytus, Dorotheus of Tyre, Jerome, Augustine, Eusebius**

and others. They all say this was a sect of licentious antinomian Gnostics who lapsed into their antinomian license because of an overstrained asceticism. Hippolytus adds that Nicolaus was the forerunner of Hymenaeus and Philetus who are condemned in 2Ti. 2:17. . . . The few ancient voices that defend Nicolaus against charges of apostasy raise some questions, but are not sufficient to negate the strain of tradition that traces this sect back to Nicolaus.'—Robert L. Thomas, *Revelation 1-7* (Chicago, IL: Moody Press, 1992), 148-149."

In Book 1 of *Against Heresies*, Irenaeus described the Valentinian Gnostic sect. He said this group could be traced back to Simon Magus, the magician who wanted to purchase the ability to baptize persons with the Holy Spirit described in Acts 8:9. In Chapter XIII of his book, Irenaeus explained that Simon continued to study magic and made himself out to be "god" (identified with Jupiter). He developed a system of thinking where a woman or mother of all things leaped forth from his mind (called Helena, also identified with Minerva) and created angels (similar to the Gnostic aeons or divine emanations), who then created the world. The angels (or aeons) detained and maltreated her. The Christ-self came to free her. The followers of Simon were mystic priests and called Simonians. Irenaeus identified their doctrines as the "knowledge, falsely so called" of I Timothy 6:20.

Halley's Bible Handbook (p. 623, 1957) tells us that Pergamum was a stronghold of the Nicolaitans. Is it a coincidence that a temple to Jupiter was erected in Pergamum, and that this city was called "Satan's throne"? We are warned in the scripture to not allow this type of thinking in the church, but to rebuke it and remove it. In addition, the epistle to the Colossians warns to beware of those who worship angels and get puffed up about their knowledge.

Revelation 2:15 says, So hast thou also them that hold the doctrine of the Nicolaitanes, which thing I hate.

II Timothy 2:17 says, And their word will eat as doth a canker: of whom is Hymenaeus and Philetus;

Galatians 1:8 says, But though we, or an angel from heaven, preach any other gospel unto you than that which we have preached unto you, let him be accursed.

Colossians 2:18 says, Let no man beguile you of your reward in a voluntary humility and worshipping of angels, intruding into those things which he hath not seen, vainly puffed up by his fleshly mind,

These are some examples of Gnostic thinking developing at the same time as the growth of the Church. These false gospels or heresies continued from the apostolic time until the time when considerable Church doctrine had been established and the gospels and epistles were canonized.

Gnosticism was incorporated into theosophy in Medieval and Renaissance times. Arendzen contends that Gnostic thinking declined in the 3rd century, and that these particular sects rapidly died out. Yet, Arendzen points out that gnostic thinking is a part of 19th century theosophy, along with aspects of it that he says were incorporated into Medieval Kabbalah, Renaissance alchemy, Jungian psychology, and existentialism. There is little doubt that gnostic thinking was adopted by the Cathari or Albigenses of 12th-14th centuries in southern Europe, who challenged the Catholic Church. They believed the good god was the God of the New Testament and the evil god was Satan, creator of the physical world (Heretics 1965). Many ideas from these ancient religions have arisen in the present and have been incorporated into New Age teachings.

The struggle of the apostles and church fathers with heresies helped them to precisely define Church doctrine. We know from Acts 15 and 21 that believers were to refrain from partaking of food sacrificed to idols and fornication, which were practices of the Nicolaitans. Let us return to Marcion of the dualist school for a minute. Marcion said the God of the Old Testament was legalistic, tribal and barbaric and was not the Christian God. It was Irenaeus' refutation of Marcion that allowed the acceptance of the two-fold canon (Old Testament and New Testament) within Christianity (p.

32, Kaminsky and Lohr 2011). We believe the God of the Old Testament was the same God as the God of the New Testament.

3c. Precreation Chaos (Modified Gap)

The two major modern theologians promoting the idea of creating from preexisting chaos (not created by God) are Bruce Waltke and R. Russell Bixler. They disagree as to whether creation of the cosmos was accomplished in a chronological six-day period or not. Bixler sees six literal days of creation beginning with Genesis 1:3 and the preexisting material is what God uses to make the universe. In contrast, Waltke is not a six-day creationist, but thinks six days represent something else.

Waltke published his thoughts about the first book of Genesis in a series of five papers (1975a, 1975b, 1975c. 1975d, 1975e), along with a commentary on Genesis with similar ideas in 2001. Since Waltke interprets the six days of Genesis 1 as a "dischronologized" framework of origins, we are not investigating his entire interpretation, just the gap that he sees between verses 1-3. Waltke also gives abeyance to scientists and the Big Bang theory (p. 25, 1975a). As reviewed by Kulikovsky (2002), the darkness and deep of Genesis 1:2 are "surd evil" in Waltke's view and describe a "precreation state."

Mark Rooker published a two-part critique (1992a, 1992b) of three views:

1) Waltke's view,

2) the gap theory,

3) and the traditionalists' view (that God created the "so-called chaos"). Rooker more than adequately defends the third viewpoint, to which he subscribes.

An excellent critique of the gap theories, especially focusing on the precreation chaos gap, was presented by John Zoschke in 2008 at the *Sixth International Conference on Creationism* (see also Zoschke 2011). Rev. Zoschke is pastor of Grace Bible Church in Garden City, KS. He cautioned that precreation chaos should be contested by creationists.

In Chapter 3 of his book *Earth, Fire and Sea* (1999), Bixler does what he calls an exegesis of the first three verses of Genesis. However, his analysis is essentially a discussion about different translations based on grammatical critiques, and a criticism of various interpretations. Bixler also argued that creation *ex nihilo* was initially proposed by the gnostic Basilides on the basis of the Zoroastrianistic zero, a great discovery; whereas because it was gnostic, this discredits it. Bixler suggests there was no concept of nothing in theological interpretations prior to 1st century; however, other sources seem to disprove that. Bixler challenges what he calls the post-Enlightenment viewpoint as an invalid appreciation of Hebrew writing. He concludes (p. 31, 1999) there must have been a precreation chaos, emphasizing his bias with statements like **"this situation [God creating chaos] is scripturally impossible"** and **"…no student of scripture without a theological ax to grind could consider a creation out of nothing to have taken place in verse 1."** Although he does not agree with it, Bixler does thoroughly present the traditionalists' view that God did create the chaos. Bixler concludes his summary by calling for God's Spirit who inspired the writing of the scriptures to help us interpret them, which in itself is commendable.

Bixler is almost convincing as he analyzes Romans 4:17 and Hebrews 11:3, speaking about what is seen being made out of things that do not appear. He suggests that "do not appear" must refer to Platonic ideals or forms, since when the New Testament was written the culture was immersed in this Greek worldview. However, the suggestion that physical things were made from spiritual things has no bearing on whether the universe was made from precreation chaos, except to dispel the connotation of creation *ex nihilo* in these verses. I would contend that these two verses from the Epistles are consistent with all things being created from nothing, as was suggested by Whitcomb (p. 41, 1972), and do not have to do with denunciating Plato.

Where did this precreation chaos come from?

Bixler agreed with Waltke in saying that the chaos was just there, and God used it to create. Bixler, in fact, references Waltke's IVth paper (p. 338, 1999) in answering the question posed: Where did the chaos come from? Bixler (p. 87-88, 1999) stated, "Simply, the Bible doesn't say." He said God "seized" this co-existent "protyle," which was "dominated by entities that are at enmity with God" and used it to create everything else. He (Ch. 9, Bixler 1999) goes on to portray God's battle against Leviathan the dragon (Isaiah 27:1) and the uncontrolled oceans (Psalm 104:7). Waltke said these passages were references to pagan mythology, but Bixler disagreed.

It seems that if this chaos was inherently evil, God being full of wisdom would not use it to create things that He would call "good" and "very good." If it had the potential to be evil, to be either good or evil, then what can we say about God creating Lucifer? There seems to be no discussion in Bixler's and Waltke's theologies of how Satan (or Lucifer) connects to this potential evil that they propose God utilized to create.

We know that God created all the angels, including those that disobeyed. As discussed previously, God did not create evil, but evil is essentially the absence of good, just as darkness is the absence of light. With the possibility of obedience also comes the possibility of disobedience. God created man with freewill, as He also created angels. Furthermore, we see in the scripture God uses even evil things or demons (e.g., a lying spirit) or Satan to accomplish His purposes. It seems Bixler, as well as Waltke, had nothing to say about creation of the heavenly heavens and angels.

II Chronicles 18:21 says, And he [lying spirit] said, I will go out, and be a lying spirit in the mouth of all his prophets. And the Lord said, Thou shalt entice him, and thou shalt also prevail: go out, and do even so.

Precreation chaos is supported by other theologians and scientists attempting to correlate these two disciplines. Support for a precreation chaos is given by Claus Westermann, a German theologian who published a commentary in German on Genesis 1-11 in 1984 (cited by Bonting on p. 251, 2005). Westermann does not translate Genesis 1:2 as the Spirit of God hovering over the waters, but sees this phrase better translated (p. 147, Bonting 2005) "a mighty wind swept over the face of the waters"; and that is a part of the precreation chaos, says Westermann. His viewpoint, like that of Bonting, allows science and theology to be speaking of the same thing. Bonting says this precreation chaos was that from whence the big bang arose. It is scientifically impossible according to Bonting (pp. 69-73, 2005) for there to be creation *ex nihilo*. He also appeals to the problem of evil, i.e., God cannot create evil, to support his idea. This was discussed in the introduction of Chapter 2, above.

Chapter 4

Gap Theories

All of the gap theories include a gap between Genesis 1:1 and the six days of creation. During that gap, there could have been the creation of the heavenly realms and/or intergalactic space and/or earth itself. This exposition is primarily concerned with these gap theories and a literal six days of creation, not other theories like theistic evolution.

The ruin-restitution gap is usually what we think of when the term gap is used. This usually entails not just a gap of time between Genesis 1:1 and 1:2, but a fall of angels with Lucifer, sometimes a pre-Adamite race of people, and often the presence of dinosaurs on the earth at that time.

The term soft gap evokes a proposed theory by Gorman Gray where outer space and the earth are created eons of time before the six days of the present creation. Gray emphasizes his acceptance of the Bible verse in a literal sense, and so calls himself and those that accept his theory Undefined Age Biblical Literalists.

Traditionalists like Martin Luther (cf. Batten 2004 who also lists Chrysostom, Ephraim the Syrian, Basel the Great, Ambrose of Milan, Calvin, Matthew Henry, and John Gill as traditionalists in his footnote #3) accepted a six-day creation, with an initial creation *ex nihilo* in the first verse. Sometimes they included a gap of undesignated time between 1:1 and 1:2, so this subgroup might also be considered to be gap theorists. In fact, numerous references to the latter with this view were perhaps faultily listed by Custance in support of the ruin-restitution theory. What they believed has been considered in the section 2c above.

Finally, the fact that angels and the spiritual heavens are believed by some to have been created long before the cosmos was created could be thought of as a gap before Genesis 1:1, i.e., a gap between creation of spiritual heavens and the cosmos.

4a. Ruin-Restitution Gap

The "so-called" gap theory most think of when they hear this term has been attributed to resolving a conflict between geology and scripture. Thomas Chalmers, a Scottish Presbyterian evangelical, advocated this view in about 1800 as geologists proposed long ages of the earth based on evidence of sedimentary layers and fossil finds, in a time of cultural acceptance of the scientific approach to discovering truth. This theory propagated (p. 68, Bixler, 1999) through J.N. Darby, the Irish founder of the Plymouth Brethren, to two others of the same denomination, the English writer George Pember (1911) and then Cyrus Scofield (1945).

The gap theory moved into Pentecostal circles via the Bible commentator Finis Dake (1961). Dake influenced present-day evangelists like Benny Hinn and Perry Stone. The well-known television pentecostal Perry Stone (2010) has a set of prerecorded lectures entitled *The Pre-Adamite World*. Evangelist Perry Stone presents seven theories about origins in these lectures, including the gap theory and young earth creationism and others. To his credit he states, "I'm presenting the information, and you have to decide." He also tells us that he has studied it for 25 years, and he thinks what you believe about it does not determine your salvation. He presents the basics of the ruin-restitution theory, and evidence against evolution and for a young earth, which would be consistent with the gap theory. Stone admits there is no evidence of pre-Adamic man.

It is ironic how the very same authors are attributed to supporting the gap theory by some authors, and not supporting it by others. Two major books critiquing this theory are those by Arthur Custance and Weston Fields. Custance wrote *Without Form and Void* (1970); Fields wrote *Unformed and Unfilled* (1976). This review will evaluate the writings of these two authors.

The gap theory was covered quite extensively by Anton Pearson (1953), Bernard Ramm (1954), Waltke (1975c), and also by Russ Bixler in 1999 (first published in 1986), among others.

Credit should be given to these authors for tracing back the origins of this gap theory; however, using support from traditionalists who did not accept a ruin and restitution of earth after the gap to support this interpretation of Genesis 1:1-3 seems unreasonable. An example of this is Custance (p. 16, 1970) citing Pererius, the Jesuit priest of 16th century, who just questioned whether there was less than a day, or more than a day, between the initial creation and the six days.

Since Pearson published first (in 1953), let us observe his views as to whence this theory arose. Anton Pearson was a theology professor at *Bethel Theological Seminary* in St. Paul, Minnesota until 1966. Pearson (p. 27, 1953) started with O. Zoeckler's entry on creation in the *New Schaff-Herzog Encyclopedia of Religious Information* published in about 1908. **"This hypothesis [gap theory] which commonly includes some traces of the partially Gnostic or Manichaean idea of the interference of Satan and his demons in the process of creation, seems to have found its first expression in the Arminian theologian Episcopius of Holland (1593-1643); its serious scientific defense was undertaken by J. G. Rosenmuller (German Lutheran, 1736-1815) in his *Antiquissima Telluris Historia* (Ulm, 1776), while at the same time and later, a number of theosophical writers used the idea in connection with the speculations of Boehme."**

So Pearson by way of this citation traces the gap theory back to Mani (216-276), the Iranian Gnostic prophet, and Episcopius of 16th century to the German mystic Boehme. Pearson also brings us through the 19th century up to mid-20th century with his additional comments, after which he vehemently disagrees with the theory. Pearson gives additional references in his footnote 65. One reference he gives is Keil and Delitzsch (1866), which is very helpful. Retracing the steps that Pearson took when he wrote this review would be advisable for those interested in how this theory materialized. Pearson (p. 27, 1953) called this theory restorationism, and he further wrote, **"The theosophists Baumgarten and F. von Meyer, and later theologians Buckland,**

Chalmers, John Pye Smith, Murphy, Kurtz, and the whole dispensationalist school represented by Scofield all adhere to Restorationism."

Incidentally, Pearson (pp. 23-24, 1953) also dealt with the existence of eternal matter; he said it was impossible because of God creating *ex nihilo*. Pearson gave evidence that Spinoza, Hegel, Schleiermacher, and the English idealists were all philosophers and not theologians in subscribing to this idea of eternal substance. The German and English idealists put forth that an eternal *divine ideal* gives rise to morality, in contrast to a Biblical foundation for morality. This is consistent with the "dualistic morality" of the Manicheans who said matter was evil and spirit was good, and morality arose from the spirit within man.

In their commentary on Genesis (p. 49, 1866), Lutheran professors Keil and Delitzsch state the three phrases:

1. earth was waste and void,

2. darkness was upon the face of the deep,

3. the Spirit of God moved upon the water, are parallel;

and all **"describe the condition of the earth immediately after the creation of the universe."** There is no gap there. It is interesting that Delitzsch converted from Jewish to Lutheran and even founded a seminary in 1866 for training in missionary work among the Jews. Professors Keil and Delitzsch go on to say, **"This suffices to prove that the theosophic speculation of those who 'make a gap between the first two verses, and fill it with a wild horde of evil spirits and their demoniacal works, is an arbitrary interpolation' (Ziegler)."**

Keil and Delitzsch then send us back to the quotation from Werner Karl Ludwig Ziegler, Protestant theologian and philologist at the University of Rostock, who published *Zur Geschichte des Glaubens an das Daseyn Gottes (On History of Faith in the Existence of God)* in 1792. It was Ziegler's contention that the gap theory was theosophy.

Now let us look at how Custance versus Fields interpret early references differently. Custance gives support to the gap theory with traditionalists who suggest some time could have elapsed between initial creation and the six days. But Fields argued there was no fall of devils or ruin of the earth in these views. Fields also showed that the ancient Jewish sources were what he called "fanciful "or "mystical," and the Medieval English poet Caedmon and King Edgar referenced by Custance did not truly have the same view as the ruin-restitution theory.

Custance (1970) made a trek back into Jewish sources: *Targum of Onkelos*, the *Book of Jasher,* the *Legend of the Jews*, and *The Zohar*. The *Targum of Onkelos* is said to be the authoritative translation or paraphrase of the Torah into Aramaic and thought to have been accomplished in early 2nd century A.D. Custance presented an unconvincing case that "unformed and void" really meant destroyed. Then Custance also moved on to Medieval England to search for antiquated sources for the gap idea, referencing the poet Caedmon of 650 A.D. and King Edgar of 950 A.D. for accepting a fall of the angels prior to the earth's creation. Then Custance moves to the traditionalists who said the six days could have come many centuries after the initial creation to support his theory, and references Aquinas and the Jesuits, Dinoysius Petavius and Pererius, both of about 1600 A.D. As a final point, Custance reaches Bernard Ramm's book and citations from 1700 and on, to Chalmers and the 19th century geologists. He goes on to argue that Delitzsch changed his mind after discussions over some years with Johann Kurtz primarily about whether "the earth was" of Genesis 1:2 could be rendered "the earth became." Delitzsch (cited by Custance p. 21, 1970) concluded**, "There is much for and nothing against the supposition that the *tohu wa bohu* is the *rudis indigestaque moles* [translated: clumsy unstructured mass] into which God brought this earth which He had first created good, after the fall of Satan to whom it had been assigned as a habitation."**

It would seem that it is not definite that Delitzsch actually did change his mind, but just allowed for an alternative interpretation.

Fields critiqued Custance's work thoroughly, delving into detail on the sources. Fields makes the case that the traditionalists may have allowed a time span between creation *ex nihilo* and the six days, but that does not imply a ruin took place in that span; and he cites Aquinas and the two Jesuits Dinoysius Petavius and Pererius mentioned by Custance in that regard. In the view of Origen of 2nd century, there was a fall of angels prior to our earth being created, but it had nothing at all to do with this earth and was not like the gap theory. Most traditionalists, explained Fields, did not have a gap at all, but considered the creation of Genesis 1:1 to be part of the first day; and Fields cited Luther and Calvin. He (pp. 38-39, 1976) also explained there was no soliciting of a gap by writers of the *Geneva Bible, Tyndale's Bible*, or the *Douay Version*. Furthermore, Fields suggests that 18th century German sources like Rosenmuller were already being influenced by geological speculations. In addition, he showed there was no written reference for the Episcopius view given by Ramm and also cited in the *New Schaff-Herzog Encyclopedia*.

Before this topic is ended, it would probably be beneficial to deal with the theosophists Baumgarten and F. von Meyer, and Boehme, in considering the gap theory; as well as the restorationalists like Scofield and Buckland, John Pye Smith, Murphy, and Kurtz, all said to hold to the gap theory by Pearson (see above). Do any of their arguments have validity? Note the above list of works is given by Custance's Appendix I (p. 7, 1970), and Pearson's review (p. 27, 1953).

Reusch, author of *Nature and the Bible* (1886, cited by Custance 1970) refers to most of these authors listed above as contributing to the discussion but not necessarily subscribing to a gap. Reusch said that Genesis shows God created everything, that man is the center of the creation, and the Sabbath should be kept holy in honor of the Creator. Reusch claimed the rest of the truths ascertained are of lesser importance.

Boehme seems to have deviated from basic Christian doctrine into what could be considered theosophy (more about him below). Siegmund Jacob Baumgarten (1706-1757) was professor of theology at Halle and deviated into rationalism. Johann Friedrich von Meyer (1772-1849) published a translation of the Bible in German. Baumgarten and von Meyer's views are not well-known, and at this point in time, extraneous.

The others in the above list were contemporaries of 19th century geology and the attempts to bring into concordance geology and scripture. William Buckland and John Pye Smith were both 19th century British theologians/geologists who reconciled the two disciplines by adhering to the gap theory. James Gracey Murphy (1808-1896) was a theology professor in Belfast who wrote *A Critical and Exegetical Commentary on the Book of Genesis* (1867). Johann Heinrich Kurtz was a German theologian of the University of Dorpat, who was interested in this issue.

J.G. Murphy (p. 5, 1867) interpreted Genesis 1:1 as being the "absolute and aboriginal creation" of heaven with galaxies and a pre-Adamite earth presumably with animals and plants (not humans). Genesis 1:2 describes the condition of the earth prior to a re-creation of animals and plants, and "in particular, man." Murphy said the Bible does not tell us how long the interval was; he concludes that questions about it are "to be asked of some other interpreter of nature than the written word." His was not the gap theory *per se*.

Johann Henrich Kurtz wrote *An Exposition of the Bible Cosmology and its Relation to Natural Science* in 1857. He left the question of whether the original creation of Genesis 1:1 was either the beginning of creation with the rest being described in the remaining verses of the chapter, or an original which was then re-created starting with Genesis 1:2. Later in his book, Kurtz makes a case that Satan and his angels had fallen prior to man, and that Genesis 1:2 could be viewed as a ruin due to God's judgment upon the original creation. Thereby Kurtz supported the gap theory and was able to reconcile the science of his day with scriptural interpretation.

There we almost have it. The gap theory historically was always peripheral to predominant Christian doctrines and weakly supported. It was revived and strengthened by theologians wanting to allow for science's ideas of creation being millions and billions of years ago.

Let us quickly consider Jakob Boehme and George Pember and their contributions to the debate. Boehme appears to have been a brilliant and original thinker who strayed from sound doctrine into philosophical meanderings and mysticism. Theosophists claim him as one of theirs (Theosophists 1938). George Pember received a Master's in Classics from *Cambridge*, and became apparently enthused about exposing theosophical inroads into Christian thinking that were occurring at the turn of the 20th century. His book *Earth's Earliest Ages* (1911, first edition 1876) ties the gap theory idea of fallen angels being judged prior to re-creation of the earth with increasing demonic activity of his day. Pember's teaching was held sacrosanct by fundamentalist teachers of the 20th century like Scofield and Dake and others that followed (see above).

As we peruse our journey through the literature on the gap theory in order to summarize, we come back to Delitzsch and prior to him, to Ziegler's conclusion that the gap theory is better related to theosophy than sound Christian doctrine. Pearson traces it through gnostic writers who claim this teaching of good and evil goes back to the beginning of mankind. (It is easily found in Mesopotamian creation myths.) Furthermore, those who have advocated for the restitution theory have provided a rather problematic list of scholarly references supporting it.

It is perhaps difficult to trace every link of the gnostic scenario into the ideas of gap theorists, but there certainly is evidence that is more than suggestive of a historical sequence. Early on these ideas were rejected, but it seems they tended to creep back into the ideas of later commentators as we have seen. Gerhard May (p. 52, 1978) author of the very thorough *Schopfung aus dem Nichts* (*Creation Ex Nihilo*) stated, **"The distinction made between a crowd of divine beings, the doctrine of the Fall, before time, of a heavenly figure, which happened before the creation of the world and first led to it; the whole mythological imagery in which the gnostic presented their teaching about the origin of** the world: all that was justly regarded as unchristian and was rejected [by early Church leaders]."

4b. Undefined Age Biblical Literalists

This type of soft gap is seen in the views of Gorman Gray, author of *The Age of the Universe, What are the Biblical Limits* (2005a). In his retirement from industry as an engineer, Gray undertook a reconciliation of the age of the universe being 14 billion years with the literal interpretation of Genesis 1 being six days of creation. Gray's view is that God created the earth and cosmos on the first day, but it was not further created for the occupancy of man until billions of years later. The gap is between 1:1 and 1:3. Genesis 1:2 describes the earth as being "swaddled" in an impenetrable covering of water, but underneath the water is the earth with its main features but no life yet.

Gorman Gray has the solar system, galaxies, and outer space created on the first day, but not visible to earth until day four. He had the earth being fully created with presumably core, mantle, and ground, but entirely submerged under deep waters. This solves the distant light problem; light from stars billions of light years away has had time to reach us. Jonathan Sarfati (1998) criticizes this idea on the basis the word *asah* is used for God making the sun and heavenly bodies in verse 1:16 instead of the word *ra-ah* for "to make appear." Sarfati reported that 20 different translations of verse 1:16 said the sun, moon, and stars were made; not that they appeared. Grigg (2001) wrote that "asah" means *make* throughout Genesis 1, and when the meaning *appear* is meant in Genesis 1:9, the word "ra-ah" is used.

In defending himself against critiques of his work written by Frank DeRemer (2005), Gorman Gray (2005b) stated that the chief disagreement was that he did not put a date on Genesis 1:1. However, it could be argued that DeRemer had three disagreements:

1) DeRemer said day one has to be a whole day, but Gray has it as only half of a day,

2) *tohu* needs to be formless not uninhabited, and

3) heavens of verse 1 refers to space, not heavenly bodies. Gray has all the outer space and earth created first, with water over the globe.

In response to these three disagreements, let us think through each one in turn:

1) The evening of day one was the darkness of verse 1:2, and that is needed to make a full day, whereas in Gray's scenario, day one begins in verse 1:3 with light permeating the waters around the earth, which makes it only a half-day.

2) Gray's translation of *tohu* is similar to the restitution theory's translation, which has been argued again and again as having connotations extending beyond its simplistic meaning.

3) Finally, the argument about heavens in verse 1:1 is worthy of consideration, due to the fact the Bible indicates the heavenly bodies were created on day four. Verse 1:16 says "And God made two great lights..." continuing on to verse 1:19 "And the evening and the morning were the fourth day." The making of sun, moon, and stars are listed as the activities of God's creating on day four, implying that these were not made way back billions of years earlier.

The arguments against Gray's soft gap theory look like they are sufficient to question its validity. Another argument could be made that the heavens of Genesis 1:1 were spiritual heavens, and that outer space was not made until day two when the waters above were separated from the waters below. Grigg (1997) seems to agree, saying that angels were created on day one. Other creationists have proposed day one as when angels were **probably** created (p. 57, Morris 1976; p. 94, Kelly 1997). Grigg pointed out that it was not necessary that angels be created ages before the six days because they could rebel even within an hour or a day.

4c. Some Traditionalists

Some traditionalists held to a soft gap between Genesis 1:1 and 1:2 or 1:3. Some traditionalists include the first verse with the six days; others have a gap after Genesis 1:1. Proving that certain authors actually conceived of a time gap is difficult. Martin Luther believed God created primeval matter in an instant, then created the cosmos in six days. Was there a gap in time between the instantaneous and the six days?

Tertullian (160-220) said (cited by Fields, p. 26, 1976) that the earth once created (Genesis 1:1) "**awaited** its perfect state, it was 'without form and void:' 'void' indeed, from the very fact that …it was still covered with waters." (Incidentally, Tertullian also had the dry land appearing from underneath on the third day as the water was withdrawn into hollow abysses, showing he believed the earth had already been created before day three.) How long did the waiting (awaiting) last? So, we could say that Tertullian might have had a gap after the first verse of Genesis. See section 5b. for more about Tertullian.

In opposition to any kind of gap between God creating material which was used to create everything else in the six days, let us recall Exodus 20 and Nehemiah 6, where the reader of the Bible is told that God created everything, all of heaven and earth in six days. This would surely include the spiritual heavens and angels too, and preclude any gap between the beginning and the six days.

Exodus 20:11 says, For in six days the Lord made heaven and earth, the sea, and all that in them is, and rested the seventh day: wherefore the Lord blessed the sabbath day, and hallowed it.

Nehemiah 9:6 says, Thou, even thou, art Lord alone; thou hast made heaven, the heaven of heavens, with all their host, the earth, and all things that are therein, the seas, and all that is therein, and thou preservest them all; and the host of heaven worshippeth thee.

4d. Re-creation Revelation Theory

Merrill Unger wrote extensive commentaries on the Bible in his handbook and dictionary. Unger held to the six days being a "dischronologized" framework for a revelation within six days to the writer of Genesis how the universe was refashioned from chaos. He calls this the re-creation revelation theory. Unger believed that chaos results from God's judgment of Satan. It would seem that creation *ex nihilo* at an earlier time was the logical choice for Unger (p. 28, 1958), because he reasoned that a perfect Creator would not initially create chaos. (But as suggested elsewhere, if the chaos is not evil or disordered in an evil sense, but just a beginning of a sequential process of creating, why not?) Unger reasoned using the assumption that God would not create chaos. Therefore God judged the fallen angels, the earth is ruined, and Genesis 1:1 begins a creation that adds man to be the overseer of the earth. Unger (p. 29, 1958) portrays earth as a globe covered with fog and mists in Genesis 1:2. When God says let there be light, the light of God penetrates the darkness. Then God continues His creating on day two in a progressive sequence of some undefined units of time represented by the word "yom" or day.

Merrill Unger (pp. 37-38, 1966) is logical in his interprettations. He is forced to put the gap before Genesis 1:1 because he says the three clauses (unformed and unfilled, darkness over the deep, and Holy Spirit hovering) are tied circumstantially to verse 1). Therefore Genesis 1:1-3 all pertain to the first day of a re-creation. Unger also acknowledges a conflict between modern science and the Genesis account, and reasoned that this idea of his would be a solution. Presumably the universe with dimensions of billions of light years would have been created way before the re-creation of earth for what Unger calls a "new order of creation – man" (p. 28, 1958).

In *Unger's Bible Handbook* (p. 38-40, 1966), Unger suggests the six days could represent either six extended epochs, or six days of divine revelation to Moses; but creation did not take place in six literal days, because that is "untenable in an age of science." He contrasts the Biblical account to the Mesopotamian *Enuma elish,* saying they are similar, but the *Enuma elish* is most likely a copy of the true account given to Moses using ancestral histories and by inspiration.

Unger had done doctoral work in Semitic languages and Biblical archaeology at *Johns Hopkins University* and theology graduate training at *Dallas Theological Seminary.* His handbook of the Bible correlates scripture with archaeological finds. He also wrote books on the archaeology *per se* that goes along with both the Old and New Testaments. His career spanned about a 19-year professorship at *Dallas Theological Seminary*, although he was a pastor of several churches prior to his professorship.

On the basis of what seems to be one scriptural passage, viz., I Corinthians 13:10, considered within its context of spiritual gifts in the Church, Unger reasoned that the gift of tongues can no longer be used validly in the Church. He stated (p. 132, 1971), **"But it is most emphatically not a regulation [do not forbid to speak with tongues] for today! It cannot be so, for the apostle has shown that tongues would stop altogether with the coming of the completed and final thing, namely, the New Testament Scriptures (I Cor. 13:10), and that prophecy (the speaking by direct inspiration of the Holy Spirit) would be superseded by a written authoritative and final revelation. Such a source for study, preaching, teaching, and edification would make apostolic prophecy completely unnecessary and tongues useless."**

The passage from I Corinthians 13:10 is probably speaking about the perfection of understanding that will come when we see Jesus face to face. Until then, we should sincerely strive for understanding, and remember our understanding may be lacking to some degree. If Unger reinforced a whole doctrinal issue on the basis of what has been argued is a misinterpretation of this one passage, then even though he is a logical man, his viewpoints on this and other issues could be considered suspect. We might construe that he is conforming his interpretation to the science of the day.

Men in many ways speak and do what is expected of them in the views of their teachers, friends, and colleagues. They do not deviate from these paths, being reinforced and constrained to follow a corridor of agreement with what is expected of them. In many cases, these are increasing compromised views that they express, hoping to please everyone. So we have many different interpretations because some Church leaders perhaps choose to head in a compromised direction instead of discerning the scriptures correctly with the help of the Holy Spirit. So instead of trying to please God, the person or commentator is trying to satisfy those persons who applaud him. When a person wants to please other men, they are in danger of committing the sin of pride.

Undoubtedly, many different interpretations exist because some are partially correct, some incorrect, and perhaps one interpretation may be correct, or maybe they are all wrong. Some authors are sincerely attempting to interpret Scripture, but due to prior indoctrinations, they miss the mark. Other authors are able to subconsciously rationalize for their success amongst their readers and students, and deceive themselves into thinking their applauded viewpoint is the correct one.

As for whether tongues are for today, we can reason that the Holy Spirit is the Comforter that Jesus promised His disciples, who will lead us into all truth (John 14:26). Jesus told his disciples to wait until they are endued with power from on high to be His witnesses to all nations (Luke 24:49). If this outpouring of the Holy Spirit that occurred on the day of Pentecost was that which was prophesied by Joel, then it was to happen in the Last Days (Acts 2:16-18). Whether we are still in the Last Days is undeniable (II Timothy 3:1, II Peter 3:3), and that we need power and teaching that occurs with the Holy Spirit's outpouring upon our lives is absolutely true. Therefore, it could be formulated that tongues would be helpful in today's world. If the rules established for the operation of the gifts of the Holy Spirit in the Church as given in I Corinthians 14 are followed, there will likely be no disorder in the assembly of believers.

Chapter 5

Early Creed

5a. Early Church and Apostle Paul

A case will be established that the apostle Paul and the early Church of his time did not believe in any kind of pre-created matter. God created *ex nihilo*. Certainly the apostle John stated unequivocally that God created all things. This would include all the angels who the Bible reveals were created by God (see Colossians 1:16 below).

John 1: 3 says, All things were made by Him; and without Him was not any thing made that was made.

Although John does not say anything about what they were created from, the beloved apostle of Christ says all things were made by the Word in the beginning, and that the Word was with God and was God (John 1:1-2). So we can reason that there was nothing at all before this beginning.

The apostle Paul in his letters to the Ephesian and Colossian churches also states indisputably that Jesus Christ was the Creator of all things, including angelic beings. The passage from Ephesians implies that this creation occurred at the beginning of the world, which is consistent with other scripture. At the beginning of time before there was anything else besides God Himself, God created. This is the doctrine of creation *ex nihilo*.

Ephesians 3:9 says, And to make all men see what is the fellowship of the mystery, which from the beginning of the world hath been hid in God, Who created all things by Jesus Christ:

Colossians 1:16 says, For by Him were all things created, that are in heaven, and that are in earth, visible and invisible, whether they be thrones, or dominions, or principalities, or powers: all things were created by Him, and for Him.

In the forward to his book, Gerhard May (p. xi, 1978) defines this doctrine as **"the absolutely unconditioned nature of the creation and specifies God's omnipotence as its sole ground."** May contends that *ex nihilo* was only well-defined when it was opposed by the Hellenistic and Gnostic ideas of creation from unoriginate matter. However, that cannot be taken to denote that Gerhard May could not visualize an implicit idea of God's creation from nothing in the Old Testament. What does the Holy Spirit tell us about how God created as we read Genesis 1? Even though not explicitly said, was there absolutely nothing from whence God created at the beginning? Genesis 1:1 and 1:2 as a complete thought would state without contest that God created every and any material from whence He created everything that followed.

Paul the apostle was believably implying creation *ex nihilo* in his letter to the Romans. It could be said that Paul wrote God called things forth that did not yet exist.

Romans 4:17 says, (As it is written, I have made thee a father of many nations…) before him whom he believed, even God, who quickeneth the dead, and calleth those things which be not as though they were.

Bixler says that in Romans 4:17, Paul is saying that God created things that exist from things that did not exist, but from things nonetheless like one would see with a Platonic mindset. He also suggests that the letter to the Hebrews contains an idea of God creating from something.

Hebrews 11:3 says, Through faith we understand that the worlds were framed by the word of God, so that things which are seen were not made of things which do appear.

Did Paul have the worldview or mindset of the Jews or the Greeks? This will be considered more later as we assess the beliefs of the Jewish scholars near the time of Jesus. Russ Bixler (pp. 49-51, 1999) has claimed that Paul and some of the church fathers conceived of creating the visible from the invisible in Platonic terms. He said the *Shepherd of Hermas* (2nd century) had this viewpoint, as did the apostle Paul. Bixler asserts that creating from nothing as an explicit concept was first seen in the writings of

Theophilus (169 A.D.) and then Irenaeus (177 A.D.). Theophilus said that uncreated matter and God cannot both be eternal and equal, but God created out of the non-existent. Bixler asks if this idea might be somewhat Platonic in meaning; that the nonexistent existed but was not seen. He went on to say that the idea of zero was a scientific idea of that early time and because of that, the idea of a preexisting nothing held sway. The ancients thought of chaos as the first thing to exist, and Bixler claims that is proven by the many creation myths that describe chaos or pre-existent material.

As to whether Theophilus had a Platonic idea of God creating from some invisible substance, nonetheless we can answer no. As elucidated by Fields (p. 26, 1976), Theophilus saw Genesis 1:2 as explaining the state of the earth due to Genesis 1:1. The entire creation account referred to the original creation in Theophilus' mind.

Bixler also suggests that Basilides, a Gnostic thinker, in point of fact came up with the idea of creation *ex nihilo* first. He said (p. 38, 1999) that Irenaeus may have gotten his idea from Basilides' heretical conception of *ex nihilo*. Basilides' ideas originated from Iranian Zoroastrianism as well as Greek and Alexandrian thinking of early 2nd century. Basilides proposed that there was a time when there was absolutely nothing. However, Irenaeus opposed Basilides in his *Against Heresies*, saying Basilides and other Gnostics, who all argued amongst themselves, felt the truth was with them alone. The Gnostics claimed they had discovered the hidden mysteries (p. 90, Bettenson 1956).

Basilides wrote his own gospel which has not been preserved, but Hippolytus of 2nd-3rd century wrote about Basilides' ideas (pp. 65-72, May 1978). Even though Basilides stated that in the beginning there existed a pure, ineffable Nothing; Hippolytus explains that his "non-being," which creates a supra-cosmic seed of potentiality (which then generates three offspring or sons—who it would seem to be heaven, space, and earth), is not the same kind of "nothing" as the Biblical view of nothing. Besides, Basilides may have equated the "non-being" with his "God," similar to the Platonic notion of God being Reason or Divine Force, a type of "non-being" but existent in the realm of the Ideals. We can conclude that Irenaeus' explicit formulation of creation *ex nihilo* he got from the Bible, not from Basilides.

Bettenson (p. 11, 1956) explained that Basilides had 365 heavens between the Supreme Being and the material world. Bettenson reported that the basic gnostic idea was that there was "One who issued Thought" which produced angels who made the world. He also believed the Nous (spirit) of the Supreme Being (or the One) descended on Jesus on the cross and then ascended immediately into heaven. Jesus was not truly resurrected in Basilides' view. There is no doubt that Basilides utilized Christian teachings as well as those from other religions, and greatly modified them to come up with his ideas. Irenaeus (p. 52, cited by Bixler 1999) was clear, **"God ... is preeminently superior to men, that He Himself called into being the substance of His creation, when previously it had no existence."**

Whether the Hebrews had an idea of zero or whether it was obtained from Zoroastrianism is debatable. It is logical that if we take away all numbers one by one, we are left with nothing. It could be conjectured that the Hebraic report in Genesis 1:2 of darkness over the deep suggests the absence of light. When something is absent, it is not there. Its presence is zilch or null. In addition, the idea of a beginning, and with the counting process not occurring until after there is evening and morning, day one, would suggest that something has to occur or come into existence and be completed in its contribution to the whole before it is counted. This argues that *ex nihilo* was implied all the time in Genesis 1. There is no reason to doubt that the divinely inspired interpretation of the creation story starts with God only and nothing else whatsoever.

The apostle Paul was Jewish and had been taught by Rabbi Gamaliel (Acts 5:34) in the school of the Pharisees (p. 235, *Smith's Bible Dictionary*). His views on creation were certainly influenced by the Hebraic teachings of the time. Gamaliel was the grandson of Hillel, who established the House of Hillel School and helped develop the *Mishnah* (written oral traditions) and the *Talmud* commentary. Gamaliel's grandson was Gamaliel II (called

Gamaliel of Yavne) who helped establish the new center of Judaism in Yavne when Jerusalem was sacked and the temple destroyed in 70 A.D. (p. 77, Wilson 1989). The strict adherence of these rabbis to orthodox interpretation of Scripture would suggest that Paul was of the same teaching. His thinking was presumably more Judaic than Greek, even though he was a citizen of Rome and able to read the Greek *Septuagint*, as well as the scrolls written in Hebrew (p. 46, Wilson 1989). The fact that Rabbi Hillel was a woodchopper and Paul a tent-maker suggests they embraced the same general worldview, e.g., that rabbis should have a livelihood outside of their teaching of the Torah (pp. 299-300, Wilson 1989).

Appreciation is extended to Russ Bixler who had provided information for and against his viewpoint. Bixler (p. 48, 1999, cites Vadja 1973) reported that Rabbi Gamaliel II had stated that God created the earth out of preexistent material, but that God Himself had created the preexistent material in the first place. So evidence is provided that this Judaic school of thought extending into the first century held a creation *ex nihilo* viewpoint.

5b. Early Church Fathers

We will consider the Apostolic Fathers (1st-2nd centuries) and the Catholic Fathers (2nd-3rd centuries) taking us into the 3rd century A.D. The author Bettenson (pp. 1-10, 1956) designates the Apostolic Fathers are immediate successors to the apostles, those being chiefly Paul, Peter, and John. The major teachers of the 1st-2nd centuries were St. Clement of Rome, Justin Martyr, and St. Ignatius. The Catholic Fathers of the 2nd-3rd centuries include Irenaeus, Tertullian and Origen (186-254). The ascetic Origen is famous for writing the six column-*Hexapla* and *De Principus*.

Karl Barth summarized his conclusions of post-apostolic theology and creation *ex nihilo* (p. 153, 1960). He states that there was "complete unanimity and resolution" about it. Barth said *creation ex nihilo* appears right at the beginning of the confession of faith of the *Pastor Hermae*, also in Tatian, in Aristides, in Justin Martyr, in Theophilus of Antioch, in Irenaeus, and in Tertullian (Barth gives all the citations of these Apologist teachers of the 2nd

– 3rd centuries, and cites Origen as well), and **"it later became one of the firmest parts of the general teachings of the Church concerning creation."**

Both Clement (died 99) and Justin Martyr (100-154) acknowledged that God created the whole universe. St. Clement is considered to have been the fourth Pope after Peter, Linus, and Anacletus (p. 2, Bettenson, 1956). His writings included reference to God as Creator. Clement (pp. 33-35, Bettenson, 1956) wrote, **"…let us fix our gaze on the Father and Creator of the whole universe," and "[Grant to us Lord] that we may hope in thy name, the primal origin of all creation…"** Justin Martyr, who was martyred in about 154 A.D., wrote in his *Apologies* (p. 59, Bettenson, 1956), **"We are not atheists, for we worship the Creator of the universe…"**

St. Ignacius' contribution was primarily speaking against heresy. Ignacius, the bishop of Antioch, was taught by John the Apostle, and said to have been taken to Rome and martyred in the Roman Coliseum by lions. The letter of Polycarp of Smyrna to the Philippians tells of the death of Ignacius and is thought to have been written in the beginning of the 2nd century (p. 33, May 1978). Polycarp speaks against corruption of the gospels by gnostic docetism. Docetism asserts that Christ only appeared to suffer on the cross, but didn't really, and so denies the resurrection. Polycarp, the bishop of Smyrna, was also taught by John the Apostle (p. 27, Fields 1976), who with little doubt was the very same person as John the Evangelist, author of the gospel of John, the epistles from John, and Revelation (Editors 1913).

The Church Fathers or Catholic Fathers are well represented by the teaching of Irenaeus, who had been taught by Polycarp. Irenaeus became the bishop of Gaul (now Lyons in France). Since Irenaeus stated emphatically that God created from nothing; this is substantial support for this interpretation being that of the apostles. Irenaeus was well integrated into the Church communities throughout Asia and Rome, and seems to have interacted with Justin Martyr and Theophilus (p. 16, Steenberg 2008).

Just who Theophilus was is somewhat of a mystery. He was a Bishop of Antioch and wrote letters that no longer exist which were cited by other Christian leaders of that time, in addition to a surviving manuscript entitled *Apology to Autolycus*. As commented on above, Theophilus said that God and uncreated matter could not coexist because God is greater, and that God created out of the non-existent. He pointed out that it is God's divine will that brings anything at all about. May (p. 156, 1978) tells us that Theophilus wrote the oldest complete commentary on Genesis, and that it was probably founded on Jewish and Christian orthodox ideas. As Bixler (p. 50, 1999) pointed out, this was the first statement by Church Fathers that God created *ex nihilo*.

Irenaeus' sound understanding of the basics of Christian faith seems to be verifiable. When explaining why God created at all, he explained that it was because of God's goodness. Irenaeus (p. 22, Steenberg 2008) wrote, **"God the creator is good, the creation itself is good, and the creative act is a manifestation of divine beneficence. Thus the 'why' of creation is bound up in the who: since God is known as creator... It is an act [creation] proper to His goodness and love to create, and an absence of creation would deny this aspect of God's being."**

I John 4:16 says, God is love; and he that dwelleth in love dwelleth in God, and God in him.

What were Irenaeus' views on creation? Weston Fields (p. 27, 1976) explains that Irenaeus wrote extensively about Genesis 1:2, and there is no mention of anything like the ruin-restitution theory in his writings. May (p. 30, 1978) reported that Irenaeus stressed the fact that God was the one Almighty Creator in his polemic against heresies. Irenaeus wrote in his *Against Heresies* (p. 154, cited by May 1978), **"God is unoriginate, eternal, needs nothing, is self-sufficient, and confers existence on everything that is... [God] who is all light, all Spirit, all substance, and the source of all good... As the Unoriginate He stands over against every originate being."**

Irenaeus refuted both gnostic and Platonic thinking, tying the Gnostics' dependence upon philosophy that derived from Plato, and that fundamentally, the cosmology of the Bible is entirely different than that of all the other cosmologies of this time period (p. 166, May 1978). Furthermore, Irenaeus expressed (p. 173, May 2008) that what God did before He created the world in the beginning is unanswerable. There remains little doubt that Irenaeus established creation *ex nihilo* as formal doctrine for the Christian religion.

Tertullian (160-225) advocated that creation by God was from nothing. He also wrote against heresies like that of Hermogenes. He said 2nd century thinkers like Hermogenes accepted "unoriginated matter" to explain the origin of evil. Hermogenes, a follower of Plato, thought the One being good could not create anything evil, so evil had to exist alongside God (p. 140, May 1978). Tertullian is famous for using the term "The Trinity" to describe "tres Personae, una Substantia" (translated three persons, one substance). His lack of explication as to whether the three persons of the Godhead were coequals or not, was one of the controversial ideas that prevented Tertullian from being canonized by the Catholic Church. Another was he aligned himself with the Montanists who believed the gifts of the Holy Spirit could direct the actions of the individual believer in Church meetings rather than the bishop's authority. Montanists also allowed women to be bishops and prophesize (pp. 42-43, Hyatt 1998). Tertullian lived in Carthage of the province of Africa. He stated that God made the world out of nothing through his Son, the Word (Wiki 2014).

Incidentally, history records that Irenaeus was sent to Rome to defend the Montanists; the opponents of the Montanists according to Irenaeus were setting aside the "Gospel and the Prophetic Spirit" (p. 44, Hyatt, 1998). So Tertullian stood with the Montanists, not against them. It has been suggested that rejection of the Montanists by the Church at that time caused a demarcation between the Age of the Apostles and a later time when revelations disappeared (p. 46, Hyatt 1998 cited Philip Schaff and Henry Wace, editors of *Nicene and Post-Nicene Fathers of the Christian Church*, 1978).

Tertullian's writings about creation are very helpful (pp. 105-108, Bettenson 1956). He expressed that God was everlasting, and that matter was created and not eternal. Tertullian said, **"Therefore that which created time had no time before time was; just as that which made the beginning had no beginning before the beginning."** In his reasoning against the gnostic thinkers Marcion and Hermogenes, he contrasts the God of the Bible with the gnostic god. The God of the Bible is good, and it is His will that this goodness become manifest. Goodness was manifested in God's creation, setting man over the earth, creating his helper Eve, creating the Law and many blessings. Hermogenes said God could not create the world because there is evil in it. Tertullian would answer that God foreknew that good would become victorious over the evil.

Origen (185-254) has been denounced as an allegorist who followed Philo and Josephus, Jewish teacher and historian, respectively. Fields (p. 21, 1976) said that Origen developed his allegorical interpretation in *De Principus*. Origen disparaged women and equated the feminine with the flesh, sounding rather gnostic – the Gnostics also believing matter and flesh were evil, only the spirit inside the man was good (p. 52, Hyatt 1998). The Gnostics also held that women were created of flesh only, whereas Paul emphasized that women and men were of the same substance. Since the Bible tells us Eve was made from Adam, this too supports the certainty of them being made of the same substance. Susan Hyatt (p. 251, 1998) wrote, **"By declaring man to be the *kepale* ('source') of woman – not the *archon* ('ruler') – Paul was denouncing the ever-present pagan notion that woman was of lesser substance than man…"**

I Corinthians 11:12 says, For as the woman is of the man, even so is the man also by the woman; but all things of God.

So what did Origen teach regarding creation? Even though Custance contends that Origen held to a type of gap or that God created heaven and earth from something else, Fields (pp. 21-25, 1976; cf. p. 9 Custance 1970) argues that Origen did not believe that. If Origen had a gap between created matter and the six days, it was certainly not like the ruin-restitution gap (see 4c). In fact, Origen pointed out that the later earth and the later heaven were not the same thing as those designated as such in Genesis 1:1. He said that had to be true if Genesis 1:1 is an introductory sentence, and not a summary statement. However, Origen believed that six literal days were described starting in Genesis 1:1, and that the age of the earth could be determined by the genealogies of the Bible; therefore there could not be a gap in his view. It was noted by Fields that Origen believed there were other worlds inhabited by angels who fell that were destroyed by God before the earth was created, but these other worlds did not include this planet. Bixler (p. 55, 1999) wrote that Origen tried to combine Christian doctrine with Platonic ideas (cf. p. 118, Runes 1959). Origen was proclaimed a heretic at the 2nd Council of Constantinople; his works were declared to be impious. His writings contained references to preexistence of souls (interpreted by some to mean he believed in reincarnation), that Jesus was subjugated to God the Father and not equal with God, and some other controversial ideas.

The conclusion that can be made about the fathers of Christianity of the first few centuries after Jesus' resurrection is that they believed in creation *ex nihilo* occurring in six literal days. This doctrine was formulated explicitly by Irenaeus in his *Against Heresies* writings in the 2nd century. Despite the controversies surrounding these two Church leaders, Tertullian and Origen also expressed that creation by God was from nothing.

5c. Jewish Scholars near Time of Jesus

Custance argued that a judgment of God resulting in a ruin of the earth before creation of the present universe was apparent in the writing of early Jewish scholars. Bixler contends for a similar type of idea of precreation chaos was in their writings. Weston Fields has evaluated some of this. We will evaluate the opinions in this regard expressed in these three books:

1) *Without Form and Void* by Custance;

2) *Earth, Fire, and Sea* by Bixler; and

3) *Unformed and Unfilled* by Fields.

Custance's sources are less valid because of a lack of direct quotations. Custance (p. 5, 1970) tells of a small mark called a *Rebhia* at the end of Genesis 1 in the *Massoretic Text* (MT) suggesting that the next word "And" in Genesis 1:2 should be translated *but* instead of *and*. Because of this, Custance reasoned that the Jewish teachers who translated this text believed there was a gap between 1:1 and 1:2. Furthermore, the *Midrash* commentaries on their scriptures hinted at a pre-Adamic catastrophe on the earth. Custance did not provide the actual quotation. The Babylonian *Targum of Onkelos* renders the Aramaic phrase of Genesis 1:2 *w' aretsah hawath tsadh' ya* to be translated "the earth was laid waste" instead of "the earth was without form and void." Custance also stated that *The Zohar* indicates there was a creation and destruction of worlds prior to Genesis 1:2 as discussed in section 1f. *The Zohar* is believed to have originated in 2nd-3rd century or as late as 11th century. These Jewish writings would not represent the thinking at the time of Jesus, but later rabbinic translations or compilations.

Custance then continues on to suggest that the apostle Paul had this understanding from his Jewish heritage, and he intimates that Hebrews 11:3 of the New Testament conveyed this understanding of a gap. Note that Paul could not have obtained this understanding from *The Zohar* because it had not yet been compiled, and the Aramaic translation may have been underway, but the *Targum of Onkelos* is thought to have originated more than 100 years later. Custance said that the passage "Though faith we understand that the world were framed by the word of God" in Hebrews 11:3 means by using the word "framed" that the earth was *restored* instead of *equipped* or *completed*. Because of lack of satisfactory documentation, and that some of the sources undoubtedly use metaphorical allusions, we lend less credence to this inference.

Russell Bixler contends that early Jewish sources speak for a precreation chaos. In his chapter "Ancient Hebraic Thought and the Concept of 'Nothing'" Bixler reminds us that those who translated the Bible were of the Greek mindset, not Hebraic; they did not translate the words "void," "nothing," or "hang" correctly. They should have translated them something like: chaos, desolation or destruction, and create. This translation implies God created out of a destroyed chaos. Bixler claims that this was the original meaning of the Hebrew text. Bixler (p. 13, 1999) says the *Septuagint* (LXX) made Genesis 1:1 a separate sentence from 1:2, but the *Masoretic Text* (MT) has it as one sentence. I think Bixler is implying that the earlier *Septuagint* conveyed a gap by having two sentences. Bixler says that so too does Rashi (11th century) and Ibn Ezra (12th century) indicate a gap because they translate Genesis 1:1-2 as something like: when God began to create, the earth was a waste with darkness covering the abyss and wind blowing over it (p. 19, Bixler 1999).

In addition, Bixler (p. 48, 1999) claims that the Jewish thinker Philo of Alexandria (a contemporary of Jesus) conceived of matter as being very ancient (or eternal) like the Greeks and certainly would not have conceived of creation from nothing. It would seem that Philo has been much misunderstood as being a Platonist. David Satran, who is on the faculty of *The Hebrew University of Jerusalem*, points out that Philo did study Greek philosophy, but incorporated it into the more authoritative Torah. Philo believed the moral (or spiritual) order and the natural order came from the same source (p. 573, Satran, 2002). Philo said that the one who follows the Law regulates his action by the will of nature according to which the whole world is governed. This sounds as if Philo held to God creating the Torah and the natural world at one time as one coherent unit.

Bixler (p. 30, 1999) moved on into six different modern Jewish commentators that have a precreation chaos view to verify that Jewish thinkers have historically held to a gap theory. However, these modern authors could very well have quite different ideas than those of early Church time.

So, Bixler's arguments are that:

1) Hebraic ideas were portrayed incorrectly due to mistranslations, and are being recaptured by Rashi and Ibn Ezra and modern Jewish theologians; or

2) Philo was able to have a Platonic view—that matter and Torah are separate because it was part of his Jewish ethos. Bixler's claims have little validity. Any such ideas of a gap are peripheral to the major stream of Judaic and Christian thought, and do not convince us that the *Tanakh* does not really mean to convey creation *ex nihilo*.

Fields (pp. 13-20, 1976) evaluates these same sources. Philo reinterpreted the Bible based on Hellenic thinking, says Fields. He also thinks that the medieval commentators Rashi and Ibn Ezra seriously departed from traditional Jewish thinking, and he points out that Merrill Unger did likewise. To support this claim, Fields (p. 18, 1999) cites the *Jewish Encyclopedia* of 1903 where Genesis 1:1 is said to represent creation *ex nihilo*. Fields says the *Targum Onkelos* does not hold to a gap, as suggested by Custance, who felt the correct translation of the Aramaic was "to be made waste," but Fields said it could be translated "to be desolate." In response to Custance's suggestion that *The Zohar* supports the gap theory, Fields replied *The Zohar* is allegorical and mystical.

The argument remains. It would appear that Fields has answered most concerns about translating Genesis 1 as creation *ex nihilo*. It is to Bixler's credit that he (p. 48, 1999) tells us that in 70 A.D., Rabbi Gamaliel II said God created something out of nothing which He used to create everything else. That the apostle Paul held this view, and was trained in the school of the Pharisees; as well as John the apostle, who was Jewish, holding this view suggests this was the interpretation given to the creation account by the Pharisees and other Judaic groups at the time of Christ. As was elucidated in the section above, there is substantial evidence that this interpretation was passed onto early Apostolic and Church Fathers, and defined precisely by St. Irenaeus in the 2nd century.

Chapter 6

Summary

Well-known Christian teachers espouse creation from nothing. However, some like Billy Graham believe the heavenly heavens and angels were created before Genesis 1:1; others say the angels are outside our time domain, and we do not know when they were created. My study proposes angels were created on day one along with their heavenly domain.

The traditional view is that God created an unformed and unfilled universe on day one (Genesis 1:1) that ends up being described in Genesis 1:2.

Some have suggested there could have been some sort of indeterminate soft-like gap between Genesis 1:1 and 1:3; for example in Martin Luther's or Tertullian's view, but it is just conjecture that this is what Luther or Tertullian meant. Representatives of the traditional view, also called the "originally perfect yet incomplete theory," are Luther, Calvin, and John Whitcomb. Any pre-atomic material created by God should not be called chaos because chaos is confused and unorganized, but material created by God is organized but not yet completely designated or formulated into its part that fits into a perfectly organized whole.

Chaos or unorganized "unoriginate matter" is that hypothesized by precreation chaos theory, Greek philosophers, or heretical gnostic sects like the Nicolaitans. Some theologians believe chaos is Satan's realm.

The Precreation Chaos (or Modified Gap) theory is represented by R. Russell Bixler and Bruce Waltke. Although not agreeing about everything, Bixler and Waltke both did say chaos could not have been created by God because it represents evil.

The objection to creation *ex nihilo* in six days is whether creation of heavenly realms and/or intergalactic space and/or earth occurred before the six days. Thomas Chalmers proposed the Ruin-

Restitution Gap Theory in about 1800, and it has been advocated in the 20th century by Bible teachers Cyrus Scofield and Finis Dake, thereby influencing vast numbers of Christians.

Professor Ziegler in 1792 and Lutheran Professor Delitzsch in 1866 expressed that the gap theory is better related to theosophy than sound Christian doctrine. Anton Pearson in 1953 traced it back through gnostic beliefs to the earliest Mesopotamian creation myths.

Gorman Gray represents the Undefined Age Biblical Literalist's viewpoint. Gorman Gray does not invoke a judgment between Genesis 1:2 and 1:3. The solar system and earth are created in Genesis 1:1. This has been called a soft gap. The arguments made in Frank DeRemer's critique of this theory are more than adequate to question the soundness of this view.

Merrill Unger's "re-creation revelation theory" has chaos resulting from God's judgment of Satan similar to the gap theory, but this occurred before Genesis 1:1. It is also different than the traditional gap theory in that the six days represent the time God took to reveal to the author of Genesis a "dischronologized" framework of how the universe was refashioned after a gap. .

The early Church apostles did not hold to pre-created matter. The apostle Paul stated that God called things that are not as though they were (Romans 4:17). Paul had been taught by Gamaliel, grandson of Hillel, who accepted creation *ex nihilo*.

The argument that postapostolic Church leaders accepted pre-created has been discredited in large part. Similarly, the argument that orthodox Hebrew rabbis of the time before Christ accepted pre-created matter has been shown to be invalid.

List of Authors or Works

Alfred, Justin T., 73

Ambrose of Milan 340-397, 80

Anacletus, {Pope} died 92, 99

Aquinas, St. Thomas 1225-1274, 59, 70, 84, 85

Arendzen, John Peter (Catholic) 1874-1954, 71, 72, 73, 75

Aristides 1st cent, 98

Aristotle 384-322 BC, 56, 59, 69, 70, 71

Ashkenazi, Yaakov Ben Yitzchak 1550-1625, 20, 28

Augustine, St., 14, 69, 70, 73

Barth, Karl 1886-1968, 56, 57, 58, 98

Basel the Great 329-379, 80

Basilides of Alexandria 2nd cent, 72, 77, 96, 97

Batten, Don, 80

Baumgarten, Siegmund Jacob 1706-1757, 85, 86

Bettenson, Henry Scowcroft 1908-1979, 96, 97, 98, 99, 101

Bixler, R. Russell 1927-2000, 70, 76-78, 81, 95-98, 100, 103-107

Boehme, Jacob 1575-1624, 82, 85, 87

Bonting, Sjoerd Lieuwe, 57, 59, 68, 78, 79

Booker, Richard, 52

Boyarin, David, 23, 24

Brown, Driver, and Briggs Lexicon, 43

Braude, Rabbi William Gordon 1907-1988, 17

Brunner, Emil 1889-1966, 56-58, 70-71

Buckland, William 1784-1856, 82, 85, 86

Butindaro, Giacinto, 45

Caedmon (Poet) 7th cent, 84

Calvin, John 1509-1564, 49, 59, 65, 66, 70, 80, 85, 107

Chalmers, Thomas 1780-1847, 81, 83, 84, 107

Chardin, Teilhard de 1881-1955, 57, 59

Christ for the Nations Institute, 50, 68

Christian Answers Net (or Films for Christ), 38

Christian Message Board, 42

Chrysostom, John 349-407, 80

Clement, St. {Pope} died 99, 98, 99

Custance, Arthur 1910-1985, 12, 28, 80-82, 84-85, 102-104, 106

Dake, Finis Jennings 1902-1987, 81, 87, 108

Darby, John Nelson 1800-1992, 81

Dathe, Johann August 1731-1791, 12

Davis, Jimmy H., 56-57, 70

Delitzsch, Franz 1813-1890, 12, 15, 82, 83-84, 87, 108

DeRemer, Frank, 88, 108

Dickason, C. Fred, 39

Didache, The, 52

Dinoysius Petavius 1583-1652, 84, 85

Dobberpuhl, Delmar, 22, 41

Dorotheus of Tyre 255-362, 73

Enuma elish, 44, 92

Envoy Magazine, 53

Ephraim the Syrian 306-373, 80

Episcopius, Simon 1583-1643, 82, 85

Eslick, Leonard J., 69

Eusebius 263-339, 73

E-Word Today, 49

Eymann, Paul E., 58

Feinberg, Jeffrey, 49-50, 61

Fergusson, David, 68

Fields, Weston, 12, 17, 42-43, 81, 84-85, 90, 96, 99-100, 102-103, 106

Films for Christ (or Christian Answers Net), 38

Finkel, Avraham Yaakov, 20, 22, 28, 44

Four Nights (Targumic poem), 23

Gabriel, Andrew K., 57

Garland, Tony, 73

Gill, John 1697-1771, 16, 61-64, 80

Ginzberg, Louis 1873-1953, 15-17, 21, 26

Graham, Billy, 39, 62, 107

Gray, Gorman, 12, 36, 80, 88-89, 108

Grigg, Russell, 88, 89

Halley, Henry Hampton 1874-1965, 74

Hegel, Georg 1770-1831, 83

Henry, Matthew 1662-1714, 63-64, 80

Hermogenes of Carthage 2nd cent, 72, 101, 102

Hershon, Paul Isaac, 20

Hinn, Benny, 81

Hippolytus of Rome 170-235, 73-74, 96

Hyatt, Susan, 101, 102

Ibn Ezra, Abraham 1089-1164, 105, 106

Ignatius, St. of Antioch 35-117, 52, 98

Irenaeus of Gaul 2nd cent, 72, 73, 74, 75, 96-101, 103, 106

Jaki, Stanley, 49, 59, 69

Jasher, Book of, 84

Jerusalem Talmud, 16

Josephus 37-100, 102

Jubilees (or Book of Jubilees), 15, 50

Jung, Carl 1875-1961, 75

Justin Martyr 100-165, 98, 99

Kaminsky, Joel S., 11, 76

Keil, Carl Friedrich 1807-1888, 12, 15, 82, 83

Kelly, Douglas, 38, 40, 89

King Edgar of England 943-975, 84

Kreeft, Peter, 25, 40, 55, 62

Kulikovsky Andrew S., 76

Kurtz, Johann Heinrich (John Henry) 1809-1890, 83, 84, 85, 86

Kushner, Lawrence, 18, 21

Lee, Brock, 14

Lindsay, Dennis, 50, 68

Lindsay, J. Gordon 1906-1973, 68

Linus (Pope) died 76, 99

Lockyer Jr., Herbert 1913-2010, 38, 62

Lohr, Joel N., 11, 76

Luther, Martin 1483-1546, 43, 59, 66, 70, 80, 85, 90, 107

Lyons, Julie, 68

Madrid, Patrick, 53

Mani (or Manicheans) 216-274, 72, 82, 83

Marcion 85-160, 72, 75, 102

Martin, James, 12, 15

May Gerhard, 56, 87, 96, 99, 100, 101

Meyer, Johann Friedrich von 1772-1849, 82, 85, 86

Midras, The, 10, 17, 104

Moltmann, Jurgen, 68

Montanus or Montanists 2nd cent, 101

Moody Bible Institute, 39

Morgenstern, Julian 1881-1977, 46, 50

Morris, Sr., Henry 1918-2006, 16, 37, 38, 89

Murphy, James Gracey 1808-1896, 83, 85, 86

Nicolas, Nicolaus Nicolaitans (or Nicolaitanes or Nicolaites) 1st
    cent, 71-75, 107

Origen 184-253, 72, 73, 85, 98, 99, 102-103

Pearson, Anton 1935-1966, 81-83, 85, 87, 108

Pember, George 1837-1910, 81, 87

Pererius, Benedict 1535-1610, 82, 84, 85

Philo of Alexandria 25-50 A.D., 24, 102, 105, 106

Plato 428-347 B.C., 56, 69, 70, 71, 77, 100, 101

Poe, Harry Lee, 56, 57, 70

Polycarp of Smyrna 69-155, 99

Ramm, Bernard 1916-1992, 81, 84, 85

Rashbi (or Yochai, Rabbi Simeon ben) 1st cent, 51

Rashi (Rabbi Shlomo Yitzchaki) 1040-1105, 61, 105, 106

Rav-Noy, Eyal, 45

Rencken, Henricus, 44

Reusch, Franz Heinrich 1823-1900, 85

Rooker, Mark F., 64, 66, 76

Rosen, Moshe 1932-2010 (and C Rosen), 19

Rosenmuller, JG 1736-1815, 82, 85

Runes, Dagobert D. 1902-1982, 103

Sailhamer, John, 12-13

Sarfati, Jonathan, 14, 88

Satran, David, 105

Sauls, Clara Haskins, 51-52, 54

Schaeffer, Francis 1912-1984, 55-56, 58, 70

Schaff, Philip 1819-1893, 101

Schleiermacher, Friedrich 1768-1834, 83

Schneerson, Rabbi Sholom DovBer 1860-1920, 17

Scofield, Cyrus 1843-1921, 81, 83, 85, 87, 108

Shepherd of Hermas (Pastor Hermae) 2nd cent, 95

Simon Magus (Simon the Magician) 1st cent, 72, 74

Smith, John Pye 1774-1851, 83, 85, 86

Smith's Bible Dictionary, 72, 97

Spinoza, Baruch 1632-1677, 83

Steenberg, MC, 99, 100

Stenudd, Stefan, 69

Stone, Perry, 81

Tacelli, Ronald K., 55

Talmud of Babylonia, 16

Targum Neofiti, 23

Targum of Onkelos, 84, 104, 106

Targumim, 23

Tauger, Rabbi Eliyahu (Touger), 17

Tatian 120-180, 98

Tertullian 160-220, 73, 90, 98, 101-102, 103, 107

Theophilus 2nd cent, 96, 98, 99, 100

Timaeus (Plato's dialogue), 69

Torcia, N. Joseph, 69, 70

Torrance, Alan, 68

Unger, Merrill F. 1909-1980, 91, 92, 106, 108

Valentinus (or Valentinian) 100-160, 72

von Rad, Gerhard 1901-1971, 66, 67

Wace, Henry 1836-1924, 101

Waltke, Bruce K., 64, 65, 66, 76, 78, 81, 107

Weinreich, Gil, 45

Wellhausen, Julius 1844-1918, 66

Wesley, John 1703-1791, 38

Westermann, Claus 1909-2000, 78-79

Whitcomb Jr., John C, 12, 45, 77, 107

Wilson, Marvin, 52, 98

Worrall A. Stanley, 56

Yochai, Rabbi Simeon ben (or Rashbi) 1st cent, 51

Ziegler, Werner Karl Ludwig 1763-1809, 83, 87, 108

Zoeckler, Otto 1833-1906, 82

Zohar, The, 50-51, 84, 104, 106

Zoschke, John, 76

List of Words or Terms

Abraham, 25, 29, 35, 61

Adam (or Adam and Eve), 25, 26, 48, 49, 60, 102

aeveternity, 40, 62

aleph, first Hebrew letter, 11, 17, 18, 21

Alpha and Omega, 11, 31

ancient, 26

Angel Michael, 16

angels, 13, 14-18, 24-26, 30-40, 50, 60-65, 72, 74-75, 78, 80, 84-91, 94, 97, 103, 107

Antinomian, 72-74

Apostolic Fathers (1st-2nd centuries), 99

Apologists (late 2nd-3rd centuries), 98

Archetypal Model (or Eternal Forms), 69, 72, 83

bait, second Hebrew letter, 17, 18

bereshis (bereshit), 11

Big Bang, 57, 62, 76, 79

Cain (or Cain and Abel), 25, 26

Catholic, 53, 55, 70, 72, 75, 101

Catholic Fathers (2nd-3rd centuries), 98, 99

chaos, 41, 43, 45, 57-59, 63-66, 76-79, 91, 96, 104-105, 107, 109

Chaos theology, 57, 59

cosmos, 18, 31, 33, 45,48, 49, 59, 60, 62, 67, 69, 76, 80, 88, 90

covenant, 9, 52, 53, 56

Creation *ex nihilo* (or *ex nihilo*), 13, 15, 55-58, 61-63, 68-71, 77, 79, 80, 83, 85, 87, 91, 94-98, 100, 101, 104, 106, 108 darkness, 15, 16, 22, 23, 28-29, 42, 44-48, 58, 63, 67, 76, 78, 83, 89, 91, 97, 105

Decalogue (or Ten Commandments), 21, 49

demiurge, 69, 70, 71

dischronologized, 76, 91, 108

Divine Light (unapproachable Light), 22, 28, 29, 30, 32, 50

Divine Throne (or throne of God), 16, 17

docetism, 99

dualism, 58

Elijah, 29, 63

English idealists, 83

Enoch, 35, 63

eretz (or haaretz), 19, 27

evil (or wickedness), 25-26, 46-48, 54, 60, 72, 75, 76, 78, 79, 83, 87, 91, 101, 102, 107

ex nihilo nihil fit, 55

Fallen angels (or demons), 24, 39, 61, 78, 82, 86, 87, 91

Feast of Firstfruits, 52

Feast of Unleavened Bread, 52

firmament, 14, 27, 33, 34, 43, 67-68

first day of the week, 51, 52, 53

foundation of the earth, 13, 17, 18, 21, 26, 32, 33, 35-39, 62, 64, 65

galaxies, 27, 33, 36, 86, 88

Gamaliel, Rabbi (grandson of Hillel, grandfather of Gamaliel II), 97, 108

Gamaliel II (Gamaliel of Yavne), 97, 98, 106

Gnosticism, 56, 58, 71-73, 75

Godhead, 13, 17, 24, 30, 101

Heaven and earth, 14, 15, 18, 20, 26, 27, 29-32, 34, 36, 49, 56, 63-67, 90, 102

Heavenly tabernacle (true temple or heavenly temple), 16, 20, 21, 29, 34, 53

Helena (or Minerva), goddess, 74

Hillel, 97, 98, 108

Holy Spirit (or Holy Ghost), 2, 4, 7, 10, 23, 24, 30, 32, 41, 52, 74, 91, 92, 93, 95, 101

I am, 21, 31, 32, 32, 42

Intelligent design, 57

Isaac, 29

Isaiah, 29, 34

Jacob, 29

Jerusalem, 98

Jewish Calendar, 52

John the Apostle, 99, 106

John the Baptist, 23

John the Evangelist, 99

Joshua, 29

Joshua and Caleb, 54

Jupiter, god, 74

Kabbalah, 28, 75

Kadesh, 54

King (or Ruler) (or Rulership), 28, 30, 31, 32, 34, 41, 60

kingdom, 7, 30, 60

Lamb of God (lamb slain), 13, 17, 22, 29, 40

Last days, 93

light, 16, 22-24, 28, 42, 46, 47, 63, 67, 91

Logos, 23, 24

mayim (or Shomayim or HaShomayim), 19-20, 25, 27, 41

Memra, 23

Mesopotamian, 44, 87, 92, 108

Messiah, 17, 21, 50, 52

Middle Ages (Medieval), 40, 51, 62, 70, 71, 75, 84, 106

monism, 58

morning, 14, 47, 48, 68, 89, 97

Moses, 10, 11, 23, 29, 49, 53, 91, 92

Neo-orthodoxy (Neo-orthodox), 56, 70

New Age, 75

new Jerusalem, 22, 35

nihil negativum, 57

nihil ontologicum, 57

nihilistic, 55

noumenal, 57

Omega point, 59

outer space, 13, 16, 27, 29, 33, 59, 80, 88, 89

parachresthai te sarki, 73

Passover, Passover Lamb, 52

Paul the Apostle, 53, 73, 94, 95, 97, 98, 102, 104, 106, 108

Pentateuch, 11, 13, 18, 20, 49, 61

Pentecost, 52, 81, 93

Pergamum, 74

Pharisees, 25, 97, 106

Pleroma, 73

Preincarnate Jesus, 29

Prime Mover, 69

Process theology, 57, 59

Proto-bodies (proto-stars, proto-moons), 22

raki'a, 19

Reformation, 55, 59, 70

Renaissance, 70, 75

rest, 48, 49, 53, 54, 61

resurrection, 51, 52, 53, 99, 103

Ruin-restitution theory, 67, 80, 81, 100, 102, 107, 108

Sabbath (or Shabbat), 31, 49-54, 61, 85, 90

Samuel, 29

Satan (or Lucifer) (or devil) (dragon) (snake), 24, 25, 26, 39, 60, 61, 67, 74, 75, 78, 80, 82, 84, 86, 91, 107, 108

Scholastics, 59, 70

seraphim, 17, 34

seven, 11, 15, 16, 17, 49-50, 72

Shekinah, 28, 44, 68

sheol, 19

Shomayim (or mayim or HaShomayim), 19-20, 25, 27, 41

six days, 11-14, 18, 27, 31, 36-38, 49, 59-61, 63, 64, 76, 80, 82, 84, 88-91, 102, 107, 108

soft gap, 80, 88-90, 108

solar system, 27, 36, 88, 108

sons of God, 37-38, 65

Sophia, 24

Spirit of God, 23, 67, 79, 83

Spirit of Jesus Christ, 23

swearing by heaven and earth, 29

Tanakh, 11, 106

temple, 9, 28, 29, 34, 53, 98

theologoumenon, 57

tithes, 20

tohu and bohu (or bohu and tohu), 15, 16, 43, 44, 45, 84, 89

Torah {Pentateuch}, 11, 16, 18, 20, 21, 49, 84

Torah {the Law}, 17, 20, 21, 22, 98, 105, 106

Traditional view, 60, 63, 107

Tree of knowledge of good and evil, 60

Tree of life, 60

Trinity, 24, 101

tzimtzum, 28

unbelief, 54, 61

Undefined Age Biblical Literalists, 80, 88, 108

Way, the, 21

waw, 12

Word, the, 23, 24, 30, 60, 94, 101

Zoroastrianism, 15, 71, 96, 97

References

5 Things You Should Know About The Zohar. 2014. Available at: http://kabbalah.info/engkab/mystzohar.htm#.VDvKZvldWSo

Alfred, Justin T. 2014. His Story through the Ages. Go to: https://www.hissongevangelism.org/ministries/seminars/index.php Choose a seminar: His Story through the Ages.

Arendzen JP. 1909. Gnosticism. The Catholic Encyclopedia. Available at: http://mb-soft.com/believe/txn/gnostici.htm

Ashkenazi YBY. 1550-1628. (1949, Printed 1885, Translated from Polish by PI Hershon). *A rabbinical commentary on Genesis ("Tzeenah Ureenah," Go Ye and Seek)*. London: Hodder and Stoughton. (This book has also been published in Hebrew, Yiddish, and French.)

St. Augustine. 415 A.D. (1982, Translated from Latin by JH Taylor). Vol. 1: The literal meaning of Genesis. No. 41-42 in *Ancient Christian writers*. NY: Newman Press.

barrykind (Member #35 of Christian Message Board). October 3, 2010. Restoration of the Sacred Name. Go to: http://thechristian bbs.com/cgi-bin/ultimatebb.cgi?ubb=search Search for: Restoration of the Sacred Name.

Barth K. 1960 (Translated into English by H Knight, GW Bromiley, JKS Reid, RH Fuller). *Church dogmatics*. Vol. III, Part 2. Edinburgh: T&T Clark.

Batten D. 2004. 'Soft' gap sophistry. *Creation* 26(3):44-47.

Bettenson H. 1956 (edited and translated). *The early Christian fathers, a selection from the writings of the Fathers from St Clement of Rome to St Athanasius*. NY: Oxford University Press.

Bixler RR. 1999. *Earth, fire and sea*. Shippensburg (PA): Treasure House.

Bonting SL. 2005. *Creation and double chaos*. Minneapolis: Fortress Press.

Booker R. 2009. *Celebrating Jesus in the Biblical Feasts, discovering their significance to you as a Christian*. Destiny Image Publisher.

Boyarin D. 2002 (2nd ed.). Logos, a Jewish word, John's prologue as Midrash. Pages 546-549 in *Essays with The Jewish Annotated New Testament*. NY: Oxford University Press.

Braude WG. 1959. The Midrash on Psalms (The second of two volumes). (Translated from the Hebrew and Aramaic Midrash Tehellim Part II, 3rd – 13th century). New Haven (CT): Yale University Press.

Brunner E. 1949 (1952, Translated from German by O Wyon). *The Christian doctrine of creation and redemption, dogmatics: Vol. II*. Philadelphia: The Westminster Press.

Butindaro G. August 6, 2010. The gap theory refuted. Available at: http://hewhohasearslethimhear.wordpress.com/2010/08/06/the-gap -theory-refuted/

Custance AC. 1957. *Bibliosymposium on Genesis (Doorway Papers No. 3)*. Ottawa (Ontario): Self-published.

Custance AC. 1970. *Without form and void*. Chapter 1. Available at: www.custance.org/Library/WFANDV/chap1.html

Dake F. 1949. *God's plan for man*. Atlanta: Bible Research Foundation Inc.

Dake F. 1991 (first edition was 1963). *Dake's annotated reference Bible*. Lawrenceville (GA): Dake Bible Sales.

DeRemer F. 2005. Young biosphere, old universe? A review of The Age of the Universe: What are the Biblical Limits? 2nd Edition by Gorman Gray. *Journal of Creation* 19(2):51-57.

Dickason CF. 1975. *Angels, elect and evil*. Chicago: Moody Press.

Dobberpuhl D. 2011. *The first four days*. Enumclaw (WA): Wine Press Publishing.

[Editors] Editors of the Catholic Encyclopedia. 1913. St. John the Evangelist. Available at: www.newadvent.org/cathen/08492a.htm

Eslick LJ. 1982. Plato as dipolar theist. *Process Studies* 12(4):243-251.

Eymann PE. 2002. Origin of angels. Christian Answers Network Website Maryville (WA). Go to: http://christiananswers.net Click on Apologetics, click on angels, Click on How did angels originate? Answer.

E-Word Today. 2013. John Calvin's Bible Commentary. Genesis 1. Available at: www.ewordtoday.com/comments/genesis/calvin/genesis1.htm

Feinberg JE. 1999. *Walking Genesis! A messianic Jewish devotional commentary*. Clarksville (MD): Messianic Jewish Publisher.

Fields W. 1976. *Unformed and unfilled, a critique of the Gap Theory*. Phillipsburg (NJ): Presbyterian and Reformed Publishing Company.

Finkel AY. 1995. *In my flesh I see God, a treasury of Rabbinic insights about the human anatomy*. Northvale (NJ): Jason Aronson Inc.

Finkel AY. 2004. *The Torah revealed, Talmudic masters unveil the secrets of the Bible*. San Francisco: Jossey-Bass.

Gabriel AK. 2014. *Barth's doctrine of creation: creation, nature, Jesus, and the Trinity*. Eugene (OR): Cascade Books.

Garland T. 2014. Nicolaitans. A commentary on the book of Revelation. Go to: www.spiritandtruth.org/teaching Click on Book of Revelation, Click on commentary, Type nicolaitans in search box.

Geneva Bible. 1599. Genesis 1:1-7. Available at: www.ewordtoday.com/comments/genesis/geneva/genesis1.htm

Gill J. 1767. A body of doctrinal divinity (divided into sections – s, of books - B, and chapters - C). Available at: http://www.ccel.org/ ccel/gill/doctrinal.html

Ginzberg L. 2008 (*Haggada* collated in 1909). *The legends of the Jews. Vol. I & II.* Forgotten Books.

Graham, B. 1994. *Angels: God's secret agents.* Dallas: Word Publishing.

Graham B. 2003. Angels were created before God made world. *Park City Daily News.* Oct. 18, 2003. Bowling Green (KY).

Gray G. 2005a (2000 1st ed.). *The age of the universe: what are the biblical limits?* Washougal (WA): Morning Star Publications.

Gray G. 2005b. A response to the Technical Journal critique of the Age of the Universe. Go to: https://theageoftheuniverse.wordpress. com/ Search for: A Response to the Technical Journal Critique

Grigg R. 1997. From the beginning of the creation. *Creation* 19(2):35-38.

Grigg R. 2001. Morning has broken ... but when? *Creation* 23(2):51-53.

Halley HH. 1957. *Bible handbook.* Chicago: HH Halley.

Henry M. 1714. *Commentary on the whole Bible. Volume I (Genesis to Deuteronomy).* Christian Classics Ethereal Library. Online. Available at: http://www.ccel.org/ccel/henry/mhc1.Gen. ii.html

[Heretics] Heretics and the Renaissance. 1965. *Theosophy* 53 (6): 179-185. Available at: www.wisdomworld.org/additional/List OfCollatedArticles/ChristianityAndHeresy.html

Hyatt S. 1998. *In the Spirit we're equal: the Spirit, the Bible, and women, a revival perspective.* Grapevine (TX): Hyatt Press.

Irenaeus. 2nd century. Against heresies. Available at: http://mb-soft.com/believe/txv/irenae1.htm and http://mb-soft.com/believe/txv/irenae3.htm

Jaki S. 1996. *Bible and science*. Front Royal (VA): Christendom Press.

[Jubilees] Pharisaic author. (2011 ed., Before 100 B.C., 1902 Translated from Ethiopic Version by RH Charles). *The book of Jubilees (or the little Genesis)*. London: Merchant Books.

Kaminsky JS, Lohr JN. 2011. *The Torah, a beginner's guide*. Oxford: One World.

Keil K, Delitzsch F. 1866 (1949, Translated from German by M James). *Biblical commentary on the Old Testament. Vol. 1. The Pentateuch*. Grand Rapids: Wm. B. Eerdmans Publishing Company.

Kelly DF. 1997. *Creation and change, Genesis 1.1-2.4 in the light of changing scientific paradigms*. Ross-shire (Great Britain): Christian Focus Publications.

Kreeft P. 1995. *Angels (and demons), what do we really know about them?* San Francisco: Ignatius Press.

Kreeft P, Tacelli R. 1994. *Handbook of Christian apologetics*. Downers Grove (IL): Intervarsity Press.

Kulikovsky AS. 2002. Disappointing discourse. *J Creation* 16(2):40–41.

Kurtz JH. 1857. (translated from German by TD Simonton). *The Bible and astronomy. An exposition of the Bible cosmology and its relation to natural science*. Philadelphia: Lindsay & Blakiston. Available at: https://archive.org/details/bibleastronomyex00kurt

Kushner L. 1975. *The book of letters, a mystical alef-bait*. NY: Harper & Row Publishers, Inc.

Lee B. 2009. *Comparative views on origins*. Prescott (AZ): UCS PRESS.

Lindsay DG. 2011. *The war on the authority of Scripture, Part 1* (Volume 17 of Creation Science Series). Dallas: Christ for the Nations Publishing.

Lockyer H. 1995. *All the angels in the Bible.* Peabody (MA): Hendrickson Publishers.

Lyons J. Dec. 1, 2006. Seven-day wonders. *Dallas Observer.* Online. Available at: http://blogs.dallasobserver.com/unfairpark/2006/12/sevenday_wonders.php

Madrid P. 2002. *Why is that in tradition?* Huntington (IN): Our Sunday Visitor, Inc.

May G. 1978 (2004, Translated from German by AS Worrall). *Creation ex nihilo, the doctrine of "creation out of nothing" in early Christian thought.* NY: T&T Clark International.

Mayim. 2014. New American Standard Hebrew Lexicon. Available at: www.biblestudytools.com/lexicons/hebrew/nas/mayim.html

Morgenstern J. 1919 (1965 reprinted). *The book of Genesis, a Jewish interpretation.* NY: Schocken Books.

Morris HM. 1976. *The Genesis record, a scientific and devotional commentary on the book of beginnings.* San Diego: Creation-Life Publishers.

Murphy JG. 1867. *A critical and exegetical commentary on the book of Genesis.* Boston: Draper & Halliday. Available at: https://archive.org/details/criticalexegetic00murp

Pember GH. 1911. *Earth's earliest ages.* Grand Rapids: Kregel Publications.

Poe HL, Davis JH. 2012. *God and the cosmos; divine activity in space, time and history.* Downers Grove (IL): Intervarsity Press.

Rav-Noy E, Weinreich G. 2010. *Who really wrote the Bible? and why it should be taken seriously again.* Richard Vigilante Books.

Renckens H. 1964 (Translated from Dutch by C Napier). *Israel's concept of the beginning, the theology of Genesis 1-3*. NY: Herder and Herder.

Rooker MF. 1992a. Genesis 1:1-3: creation or re-creation? Part 1. *Bibliotheca Sacra* 149:316-323.

Rooker MF. 1992b. Genesis 1:1-3: creation or re-creation? Part 2. *Bibliotheca Sacra* 149:411-427.

Rosen M, Rosen C. 1976. *Share the new life with a Jew*. Chicago: Moody Press.

Runes DD. 1959. *Pictorial history of philosophy*. NY: Bramhall House.

Sailhamer JH. 2009. *The meaning of the Pentateuch, revelation, composition and interpretation*. Downers Grove (IL): Intervarsity Press.

Sarfati J. 2003. The numbering pattern of Genesis. *J Creation* 17(2):60-61.

Satran D. 2002 (2nd ed.). Philo of Alexandria. Pages 572-574 in *Essays with The Jewish Annotated New Testament*. NY: Oxford University Press.

Sauls CH. 1976. *The Christian Sabbath*. Sanford (FL): Self-published.

Schaeffer FA. 1968. *Escape from reason*. Downers Grove (IL): Intervarsity Press.

Schaeffer FA. 1972. *Genesis in space and time*. Downers Grove (IL): Intervarsity Press.

Schneerson Rabbi Sholom DovBer (1892-1920). Translated from Hebrew by Eliyahu Touger). Isa B'Midrash Tehillim, Part II. 3rd – 13th century. Brooklyn (NY): Lubavitch World Headquarters. http://www.chabad.org/library/article_cdo/aid/57393/jewish/Isa-BMidrash-Tehillim-Part-II.htm

Smith's Bible Dictionary. 1979 (Revised ed.). Nashville: Holman Bible Publishers.

Steenberg MC. 2008. *Vigiliae Christianae, supplements: Irenaeus on creation: the cosmic Christ and the sage of redemption.* Boston: Brill.

Stenudd S. 2000. The Greek philosophers on myth and cosmology: Plato. Available at: www.stenudd.com/greekphilosophers/plato. htm

Stone P. 2010. The pre-Adamite world (2 CDs). Cleveland (TN): Voice of Evangelism. See: www.voe.org/store/2cd317-the-pre-adamite-world

[Theosophists] Great theosophists – Jacob Boehme. Volume 26. No. 9. July, 1938. (Pages 386-392). Available at: http://www. wisdomworld.org/setting/boehme.html

Torcia NJ. 1999. *Creation ex nihilo and the theology of St. Augustine.* NY: Peter Lang.

Unger MF. 1958. Rethinking the Genesis account of creation. *Bibliotheca Sacra* 115:27-35.

Unger MF. 1966. *Unger's Bible handbook.* Chicago: Moody Press.

Unger MF. 1971. *New Testament teaching on tongues: a biblical and historical survey.* Grand Rapids: Kregel Publications.

Vincent S. 2014. Answering objections to creation *ex nihilo* in six days. CRS Quarterly 51(1):58.

von Rad G. 1972. *Genesis: a commentary* (translation from German of *Das erste Buch Moses: Genesis).* Philadelphia: The Westminster Press.

Waltke BK. 1975a. The creation account in Genesis 1:1-3, Part I: Introduction to biblical cosmogony. *Bibliotheca Sacra* 132:25-36.

Waltke BK. 1975b. The creation account in Genesis 1:1-3. Part II: The restitution theory. *Bibliotheca Sacra* 132:136-144.

Waltke BK. 1975c. The creation account in Genesis 1:1-3, Part III: The initial chaos theory and the precreation chaos theory. *Bibliotheca Sacra* 132:216-228.

Waltke BK. 1975d. The creation account in Genesis 1:1-3, Part IV: The theology of Genesis 1. *Bibliotheca Sacra* 132:327-342.

Waltke BK. 1975e. The creation account in Genesis 1:1-3, Part V: The theology of Genesis 1 - continued. *Bibliotheca Sacra* 133:28-41.

Waltke BK, Fredricks CJ. 2001. *Genesis, a commentary.* Grand Rapids: Zondervan.

Whitcomb Jr JC. 1972. *The early earth.* Nutley (NJ): Presbyterian and Reformed Publishing Company.

[Wiki] Wikipedia Editor. 2014. Tertullian. Available at: http://en.wikipedia.org/wiki/Tertullian

Wilson MR. 1989. *Our father Abraham, Jewish roots of the Christian faith.* Grand Rapids: William B. Eerdmans Publishing Company.

Young EJ. 1976. *In the beginning.* Carlisle (PA): The Banner of Truth Trust.

[Zohar] Rabbi Simeon ben Yohai 2nd century (unspecified authorship, or Moses de Leon 13th century). (1933, Translated from Hebrew and Aramaic by H Sperling and M Simon). *The Zohar, Volume I.* NY: The Soncino Press.

Zoschke J. 2008. A critique of the precreation chaos gap theory. Pages 55-70 in AA Snelling (ed.). *Proc Sixth Interntl Conf Creationism.* Pittsburgh: Creation Science Fellowship.

Zoschke J. 2011. The three gap theories of Gen. 1:1-2. *Voice* January/February 2011:29-31.

You may contact the author by sending a request to
publisher@marjimbooks.com.

Other good books are available at www.MarJimBooks.com, home
of books bearing the UCS PRESS imprint.

UCS PRESS

Small press. **Big reading value.**

www.ingramcontent.com/pod-product-compliance
Lightning Source LLC
LaVergne TN
LVHW021513080426
835509LV00018B/2501